The Man Who Came to London

Written by A. S. Cookson

In association with

The Man Who Came to London

Published in London by Peaches Publications, 2017.
www.peachespublications.co.uk

The moral right of the author has been asserted.

British Library Cataloguing in Publication Data: A catalogue record for this book is available from the British Library.

ISBN: 978-0-9554890-5-1

Book cover design: Peaches Publications.

Typesetter: Winsome Duncan.

Proof reader: Joanna Oliver.

Dedication

This book is for Taleah Cookson (USA)
And Ezekiel Robinson (UK)
-Grow to love learning

Acknowledgements

This project has become a document in the public domain due to the role of some close friends and family who have been an inspiration at different stages.

My gratitude to those friends who read the initial chapters and willed me to write a bit more. Not believing my memoirs to be anything more than my memoirs, I was motivated by their comments and their eagerness to read the completed story. Hence, *"The Man Who Came to London"* has been completed and made available for general reading, and listening, where applicable.

Two of my colleagues who are published authors, Ruth Pearson, "Say Yes to New Opportunities" and Andrew Beckford, "A Boy's Cry", provided me with insight into the world of publishing. They shared their knowledge, experience and 'best tips' with me and to them, I would like to extend "Thank you".

I also thank fellow author, Barbara Anderson, who introduced me to the staff at *Peaches Publications*; Winsome Duncan has been the final link that I needed to turn my manuscript into the book that you are now reading. *Peaches Publications* took on the intricate task of typesetting, designing and making the final product ready for the world.

Finally, to my wife Sandra, who has been the quiet motivation for my writing and has also made invaluable suggestions throughout the writing process, assisting with research of some material. She now works as my public relations consultant, in the merchandising and promotion of the book.

Preface

The idea for 'The Man Who Came to London' came about primarily as a pastime, based upon a belief that the reality of British society has been captured and told by different voices, through various channels. Newspapers and television make their presentation in a style of their own but I wanted to tell the story in a way that reflects my origin and ethnic perspective. My earliest memories and recollections of the UK stem from tales told by the pioneers who made the journey to Great Britain, in the Twentieth Century, to fight in wars or to help rebuild London and other cities after World War 2. The face of the UK had changed by the time I saw it for myself and pushed by my initial views, I felt an intrinsic coercion to write things down as a part of my memoirs.

Bearing in mind that some travellers preserve their memories by taking photographs, others by writing poems or by collecting exotic souvenirs, I chose to preserve mine as a written log. Initially, I shared it with a few friends who said they wanted a bit more, so I obliged and wrote a bit more. I shared it again and they said they wanted to hear a bit more and that is how the whole thing got out of hand; that's how we end up here today.

Mainstream media does a fantastic job in highlighting the geography, culture and other attributes of different countries. While that is so, I still believe that there are aspects of day to day events in British society that go unmentioned. Reports in the daily papers and magazines, about Caribbean migrants in general and the Jamaican Diaspora, in particular, are usually highlighted if the story is sad, bad or mad. So, the question was then - Who is highlighting the quiet, every-day, routine, intriguing, unheralded stories that unfold and involve the hard-working and law-abiding migrants from the Caribbean?

The reaction after the exposure of my memoirs to close friends and family, was the answer to my query; for only then was it clear to me that much goes by in the regular run-of-the-mill, that is fascinating and worthy of posterity. The inherent hope and aspiration from this project is for such matters that are neither sad, bad nor mad, to be noticed and that the Diaspora can be seen for what it is truly worth.

It may be that 'The Man Who Came to London' may be used to inspire further enquiry and discussion. Hence, some potential questions are included on pages 227-229, and are intended not to hinder reflective capacity, but to initiate the reflective process.

Introduction

January 1948. A little village in Hanover. Population: around 200 people. A predominant farmers' village. No pipes with running water. A few goats. Some cows. A plot of land with ground provisions. Yam was king, banana was prince and the residents welcomed the opportunity to migrate to the 'motherland'. Ossie, Benjy, Manny and Aston could not resist the thought of a new life in the UK.

The news had spread fast around the Island of Jamaica, that the 'motherland' was recruiting workers from the Commonwealth countries to help rebuild Great Britain at the end of World War 2.

"Benjy, don't you hear the news?" asked Ossie, who was a neighbour of Benjy's.

The neighbourhood network was close-knit. It was normal for a dwelling house in that Hanover village to be within a hundred metres or less, from one another. Everyone knew everyone who lived in every community for up to five miles away, in every direction. Hence, any news – of course by word of mouth - was quickly shared with everyone in the community.

"I just heard from someone down by the shop that workers needed to go fo work in Inglan," Ossie continued. "They sendin a big ship called Empire Windrush."

The UK was not a term that was used. England was the local word as the colonial relationship between Great Britain and the Caribbean was in full swing. England was the name that was spoken; of course, with the local phonetic sound.

"I am not sure but I believe that it would help me to work some money, so I think I will sign up to leave on the ship," declared Benjy.

"My uncle was there in Inglan during the war. He was demobbed when the war was over but he said Inglan was alright," Benjy concluded.

Across the Caribbean Island of Jamaica, men and a few women, were making themselves ready to respond to the new recruitment of workers to take up jobs in the UK. Migration to the UK after World War 2 has its genesis in 1948 and the exodus continued in the following years. Neither Ossie nor Benjy knew then, that their conversation would help to form the backdrop for what was to develop as we speak – in the New Millennium.

Much has been documented about the first set of migrants who braved the unknown and travelled to a country that was no more than a socio-political reference in their local communities.

And so, the years rolled on by and more and more people from the Commonwealth Caribbean made the trip into Great Britain. All the time the background to the movement was similar, as job opportunities were available in the health sector, transport, construction and delivery services. The 1950s, 60s, 70s, 80s and 90s wooed the Islanders. Simultaneously, there was a regular return stream of Islanders, who had achieved their objectives in the 'motherland' and were returning home.

The reason for migrating and the pattern of migration, was driven by a desire to make a living that would hopefully change the economic standard of life in the colonies. Unfortunately, the views towards the migrants in the 'motherland' were largely stereotypical and forged by a misunderstanding of the Islanders; deliberately and sometimes formed out of ignorance. The reason for migration continues today, albeit, on a much-reduced scale.

The end of the Twentieth Century was to signify a new beginning - a continuation perhaps - of the movement of Caribbean people to the UK. In the Twenty-first Century, there is a new reason for migrating and so the story takes on a new twist for "The Man Who Came to London" in the New Millennium.

Chapter 1

The Cat and the Fiddle

(This chapter is dedicated in part, to the memory of Mrs B)

"Stand up straight, hold your head up," said Mrs B. It was the voice and command that they all dreaded.

"Now sing up the scale," she dutifully continued.
In some kind of unison, they began: "Do re mi fa sol la ti do!"

"And now down the scale," she ordered.
"Do ti la sol fa mi re do," they responded, at least those who could remember the notes backwards in order.

Whoever was unable to repeat the notes backwards in order, skilfully mimed something. Whatever it was that they mimed, it made their mouth appear to be in sync with the voices around; they got away with it, but not for long. Mrs B would go close to listen to them individually. She would soon discover the selective mutes, much to the amusement of the others.

Mrs B was the headmistress; Mrs Merle Blakecroft,

4

whose constructive ideals, shaped Freddy's thinking from an early age.

"I am sending you to a university," she once told him.

Freddy was no more than five years old at the time. Among the many things he learned from Mrs Blakecroft, were interesting facts and some strange fables about the United Kingdom.

Now while many of Freddy's childhood friends became interested in travelling to the United Kingdom, he did not. The thought of leaving his country of birth to travel to a more developed country was nothing that he held in his mind, except for fleeting moments as a teenager. He had vicariously lived the foreign experience as, as it turned out, Freddy was fortunate to receive a good education, despite the numerous economic challenges in the Commonwealth Caribbean. Things were never easy. There were always school fees to be paid, text books and exercise books to be bought, uniform, lunch money and daily bus fare to deal with; there were no government subsidies available nor handouts for children in school.

During his primary education, Freddy had to join in chorus and sing the nursery rhymes that were all based on the educational hand-me-downs which made reference to weather, lifestyles, customs, diseases, events and places in Great Britain. These references had no direct bearing on his local Geography and culture. So, you might imagine his robotic sing-a-long to *"Ring A Ring O' Roses"*, *"Sing a Song of Sixpence"*, *"One a Penny, Two a Penny, Hot Cross Buns"*, *"London*

Bridge is Falling Down" and *"The Grand Old Duke of York"*.

No one knew how the Grand Old Duke of York gave commands to his soldiers. Were commands given in the form of a relay? For, if the Grand Old Duke of York gave a command to the soldier at the front of the queue and that soldier, turning to his left, repeats the command for the soldier behind him and that soldier does the same, by the time the command is relayed to the ten thousandth man; a few hours later that day, it is possible that the command could be no longer relevant. It cannot be concluded either that the commands were shouted from a megaphone, as the vastness of the Yorkshire Dales might drown out the sound, petering it out into imperceptibility.

Then there was Freddy's stand-up performance of *"Little Boy Blue"*, *"Old King Cole"* and *"Simple Simon who met the Pie Man";* he recited the lines to the latter so eloquently and vigorously that you would think he actually knew the 'Pie man' - or better still, knew the taste of pie - which he did not. His favourite, however, was *"Harry went to Hampstead - Harry lost his Hat"*. The shape, size and colour of the hat remained unknown, so, what were the odds, that if someone chanced upon a lost hat, that he or she would be in any way sure that it belonged to Harry?

Freddy was comfortable with reciting. He was a natural. It was such nursery rhymes and jingles, that made Freddy feel as though he had seen the changing of the British seasons and experienced the view of the Shires, the Dales and the Meadows in a subliminal way, and made him disinclined towards moving to see them.

Freddy later learned about the experience of using the trains in Great Britain, through a poem by an English writer, commemoratively describing the station as the train approaches and the journey that last for many miles. Some Caribbean Islands had a train service after Independence, however, this soon ceased to exist. The limited antiquated service, wherever it existed, could not be compared with the miles and miles of high speed trains that thread the length and breadth of the UK.

Freddy's knowledge of Great Britain got even better as he studied Geography and Economics at A' Level in Jamaica. These disciplines were based on the British Examination system, of course, using British references. Studying at age 17 and driven by his ambition to learn and adopt a thinking and appreciation of the British Economic model, he began to understand marketing, profit and loss and trading procedure of some of the big corporations in the UK. 'Lloyds bank' was one and 'Marks and Spencer' was another.

Alas, 'Lloyd' was a local farmer - Maas Lloyd - as he was locally known. That was what Lloyd meant to him. And then he had to analyse spreadsheets with business reports from 'Marks and Spencer'. Freddy certainly knew Mark; they played football together. And Spencer was the surname of the girl who could run long distances; she won the cross country at school for five years in a row. That was the kind of distance there was between the academic references and the local reality. His task was now to dig deeper into the geography, economy and culture, an exposure which further created the vicarious experience of living and experiencing life in the UK. Freddy had no desire to see any of this first-hand. He was experiencing life abroad through studies.

A knowledge of the Second World War was part of the academic flight path to an Arts degree at the local university. This was a hot topic in A' Level History. The exploits of Great Britain against the Axis powers were taught in great detail. Students had to learn about: the strategies of the British, the nightly raids on London by the German Luftwaffe, the Americans joining with the Allies and the top-level meetings between the Allied forces. In all of this, Sir Winston Churchill was a name that recurred frequently in those hours of scholarly endeavour.

Those hours of learning went beyond the UK to Japan, the USA, China and the USSR. There was so much learning about the relationships and battles between Great Britain and other countries that it further brought Great Britain home to Freddy. Then there was Geography. The students were snowed under to hear so often of the Brecon Hills in Great Britain. Freddy endured several hours of aching joints up and down those hills while sitting at his desk. The Thames River was also in the melee, jostling for a place to stand out in his mind as a physical feature of Great Britain.

These lessons on physical features were rivetingly wearying, as they were usually just before lunch. It was just one of those nightmares for the unlucky imparter of knowledge who had her Geography lesson just before lunch time. She was seemingly punished by having to suffer the quiet disturbance from the canteen. An unfair competition for attention of sorts, as having the piquancy of freshly cooked dumplin and chicken wafting down the hallway, around the corridor and into her classroom, was some kind of distraction. A distraction that put paid to pedagogy - well until the next lesson.

Great Britain was full-on. It was a ubiquitous British diet. It was a three-course meal served through Economics, History and Geography and Freddy had his fill daily.

Chapter 2

The Countdown

Some years later and with a change of heart and mind, Freddy began to harbour thoughts of migration. This was triggered, perhaps, by the socio-political and economic environment that he had experienced locally. He had come to know it well. He worked in it. The sentiments of the UK were ongoing. Freddy believed that he had escaped - there was no more British fascination formed through the plethora of nursery rhymes that was being served up in his primary school. There were no more reminders served up through A' Level education, where the features of the economy, politics and geography of Great Britain, formed a kind of staple.

Now it was the turn of work colleagues to pick up the baton and they made their love of England known. The cricket fans made sure of that, as you would not go for very long without a cricket home series against England. When the West Indies were not hosting, they were away to England for a series and so cricket talk was perennial. How could he escape? The updates were scholarly mulled over and fervently discussed all around Freddy. England was there again, like a Greek olive wreath upon his head; sitting there, circumnavigating his head.

Now, on a different day at a different time, you may want to hear of the nail-biting encounters between England and the West Indies cricket teams; statistics, reviews, commentaries and team sheets. Suffice it to say, this may not be the right time in your day to bog you down in the intricacies of cricket. But spare a thought for those who play the game. There are two sides that play the game. The side that has eleven players out on the field tries to get the side that is in bat, out. So, when the side that is in gets out, all eleven of them, they then go out, on the field and try to get the side that is in bat, out and this mind-boggling piece of illogic can go on for five days. When you go out to bat, you get out - a bit of a conundrum as you are already out and when you get out, you are then required to come back out. This is cricket, lovely cricket.

And when it was not cricket providing the reminder about England, it was football. A football discussion was never far away at the workplace. It was usually the *Blues,* the *Reds,* the claret-clad *Hammers, Pompey,* the *Gunners* or one of several other favourites that enlivened the debates at lunch time and after work. Then there were the British expatriate workers, whose presence reminded everyone of the 'motherland'. Perhaps these perennial reminders were part of the catalyst that made Freddy reform his thinking on going to see first-hand, what lay, in reality, in Great Britain.

*****

With the shift in his Great British personal-experience-ambition-compass, Freddy decided to follow those early pioneers who had journeyed from Jamaica some five decades earlier, to Great Britain. As it turned out, the circumstances in his time were somewhat similar to what existed decades earlier. It was now a New Millennium. Great Britain was in need of professional employees. The 'motherland' needed teachers.

Bear in mind that by this point in time, Jamaica, like many other Islands in the Caribbean, was no longer economically nor politically dependent upon Great Britain. However, the Islands remained a part of the Commonwealth and maintained some allegiance to "Queen and Country"; for how long, is anyone's guess.

With the British invitation for teachers, Freddy, who worked as a teacher, had a social and professional decision to make. A choice between old friends and potential new friends had to be made. Wait, it was not as simple as that, as emotions had to be measured and weighed and economic preambles had to be judged. It was difficult to be fully prepared for such a sojourn, as a daunting five-thousand-mile journey separated a dream from reality. Getting to Great Britain was also an expensive proposition; for the local currency was weakly devalued against the pound sterling.

Quick communication with earlier sojourners was limited to a telegram. Telegrams were sent from a post office and had to be worded to a minimum. The cost of a telegram was determined by the word count. Freddy would be foolishly optimistic to believe that he could get a clear update about how to prepare for life in the UK by a telegram from those who had made the journey previously. A letter would contain more information from overseas, but a letter making a round trip to the UK and back, could take as long as five weeks.

The intrepid Freddy had gathered what information he could from family members, whenever they came to visit from the UK. Their reports were never consistent. He got glowing recommendations for England from some and a picture of hardship and woe from others. Freddy formed his opinion amidst the contradicting reports and consequently made his mind up. This enterprising teacher had had enough of the nursery rhymes and was ready to exercise the option of going to Great Britain, as it could be a world of great expectations and possible explorations. If the academic topics were accurate, Great Britain could present a world of opportunities. If the cricket and football fervour and popularity was real, Great Britain was the place for him, being an astute sports pundit.

It was now the New Millennium. The main mode of commercial travel had changed and the Jumbo Jet had replaced the boat. Go back a few decades and the

Caribbean sojourner would be bracing himself or herself for a long day at sea. A day that would turn into a week and a week would become three. Many a sea sickness, and many a yearning soul would wish to turn back or reach England fast.

In contrast, modern air travel has done wonders for this journey. It now means that in less than half a day, a journey to the UK can be completed - with hours of daylight to spare. From the rocket-like speed of the new jet-liners along the runway, front landing gear lifting away, followed soon after by the rear landing gear and passengers are airborne. Save for the inevitable popping of the ears, as the air pressure falls on an aeroplane, the modern-day mode of travel is a pastime when compared to the three-week-long torpidity of motion sickness on the ships carrying the first arrivals.

Furthermore, the dress code then was something to behold. The old photographs taken at Tilbury docks in 1948 are still around in libraries and archives. A formal attire of suit, tie, ironed shirt, polyester trousers to complement and shoes polished to perfection. *Haven't seen a pair of shoes polished that way lately.* Such was the attention given to detail and the effort made by the first batch of Jamaicans who made the voyage to Great Britain. They knew they were going to the 'motherland' and the ethics of the day dictated that they had to 'dress to impress'. For all intent and purposes, they were set to make an entrance – an entrance that has impacted Great Britain to this day.

The formal attire worn then has been replaced by a more casual kit. It would not be uncommon to hear the squeaking of trainers along the walkway coming into the arrival lounge at Heathrow, in the New Millennium. Trendy polo shirts and denims have replaced the formality of a tie, polyester trousers and jackets, as worn by the men who made their entrance into Great Britain by sea.

It was a matter of time before what seemed improbable had become a closer possibility. Freddy was forced, pushed even, by a stifling effect - an inertia. This stagnation was replaced by a need to grow, to go, to walk into a different kind of probability and possibilities. He set a quest to see a different kind of politics and philosophy at work and maybe see the snow in all its whiteness. Summer was almost over and the new school year was starting soon in Great Britain. Freddy was recruited to teach in Great Britain. He packed his bags.

Chapter 3

The Arrival Desk

The air was misty and visibility so poor that Freddy could barely see beyond a hundred metres, looking down from the window of the aeroplane. From an angle of forty-five degrees, he could just make out houses leaning sideways and the green landscape leaping up towards the clouds that hung heavily above Heathrow.

This was England. This was his new home. The feeling of great expectations filled his lungs as with each fall in altitude, he became more apprehensive of what truly lay beneath the misty canopy that hung over London. The wait to descend beneath the mist, for only then a clear view of the city would be discernible, was prolonged.

"This is your captain speaking, we have arrived over London
earlier than expected," came the voice over the intercom system. The flight-weary passengers took the

announcement with some indifference as for one, a flight getting to its destination well ahead of time owed credit to the efficient baggage loading, passenger boarding, pushback and navigational skills of the flight crew. But at the same time, arriving earlier than expected, meant that London would have to wait a while longer. So close and yet so far. As the aeroplane went around in circles, Freddy marvelled at the aircraft, such a colossal mechanical wonder, and how it stayed aloft. He concluded that the entire achievement of the aircraft to stay suspended on a cushion of air was nothing short of a miracle. Two hundred and eighty passengers, five hundred and sixty suitcases, hand luggage, trolleys loaded with food, water, duty free goods and the weight of the jumbo jet itself, ought to be a seriously heavy lift.

"The controller has instructed me to keep flying around until the space is clear for us to land," the flight captain continued, interrupting Freddy's thoughts. *"Hopefully, this won't be too long and we should be touching down at Heathrow shortly,"* he added.

The passengers had all expected to hear from the captain again when he got the signal to descend onto the runway, however, no such warning came. He, they deduced later, knew that all seatbelts had been fastened long before the landing had been put on hold and felt no need to make any further announcement about landing. The landing gear was lowered with some noise and Freddy's stomach made that uncontrollable heave caused by the sudden drop in altitude. Soon they were taxiing to the arrival gate. There is no memory of the gate number, as that information has been eroded with time.

Some minutes had passed and the queue of arriving passengers twisted and turned around the pillars and roped passageways, leading up to the arrival desk. It was hard not to sense the tension. Sniffer dogs. Roving Inspectors. Watchful eyes. Numerous CCTV cameras. Long queues.

"I hope the ackee I am taking don't go off," lamented the woman, mid-fifties, who stood behind Freddy, clutching a bag under her arm. She also had a small wheeled suitcase that was her cabin luggage, for in those days the shape and design of cabin luggage was changing from a soft bag that could be pushed and squashed into the cabin compartment, to mini suitcases. Suitcases were now appearing in cabin-friendly sizes.

"I not worryin about the breadfruit 'cause that roast yesterday," she continued, "and yellow heart breadfruit will keep long," she added.

Freddy was not sure what to say to her as, while he could share her concern for the health and safety of her breadfruit, he had concerns of his own for his baked confectionaries that were somewhere inside the airport, waiting at baggage collection.

"They will be alright," he said to console her.

"I hope so," she retorted.

"Did you freeze them before you packed them?" he asked, trying to appear genuinely concerned.

"Yes, ma dawta put them in the freezer overnight so they're well frozen," she explained.

They were soon jolted back to the moment and space

in which they were standing. The sniffer dogs were now running egotistically along the queue as the passengers, arriving from the 'weed capital', were sniffed lordly by the dogs. The dogs lost no time in their search for a certain plant. It was no wonder that the dogs would smell the fish and bammy that many passengers had wrapped carefully in aluminium foil in their hand luggage. However, despite how tightly wrapped these packages were, a bit of oil was sure to seep out at the folds. The rich marinated flavour seeped out too. No one may ever know if those canine sniffers will over time, take an addiction to the smell of bammy, ackee and salt fish, for this was a regular smell that they would encounter when sniffing Jamaican luggage.

The arrival experience of Twenty-first Century migrants was so different from the pioneers who came on the *Empire Windrush*. In 1948, Britannia ruled the waves but the business ties between Great Britain and Jamaica eventually slackened as there were reports of the illegal trade of a certain plant. The plant is believed to have been concealed in clever ways and illegally smuggled into the UK from Jamaica. This explains the unceremonious scrutiny of passengers who arrived into the UK in the New Millennium. A most undignified subjection that a guest arriving had to endure.

As the sniffing dogs continued their prancing and whimpering, Freddy could not help thinking about the food items that most passengers were carrying. The food was a little piece of 'yard' to keep the memory alive; at least for a few days until uncles, aunts and cousins have been given their share and it is all devoured.

As he left the arrival desk and walked into the interior to collect his luggage, he looked at the advert for a concert at the Lyceum Theatre, in the West End of London. The advert was shown on an electronic advertising screen, inside the airport. The Lyceum he remembered, was the concert venue where Bob Marley had his epic performance of *'No Woman no Cry'* recorded. For that, Freddy thought he would visit The Lyceum Theatre at some point. Perhaps, he would go down to Banbury Cross to see if the fine lady from the folktale was still around there on her white horse, or see if she had upgraded from a horse to a Volkswagen Golf.

Now what Freddy was not told by his receiving party, deliberately or inadvertently, was that the shade of daytime London was 'black', which he found out soon after leaving the airport. The air was misty and bleak clouds hung over them, as they journeyed from Heathrow along the motorway into the City. Piccadilly Circus. He remembered this unusual name. Bob Marley - yes, he went down to Piccadilly Circus 'where (he) saw Marcus' in one of his songs.

The automobile journeyed on. Mayfair, Trafalgar Square and Regent Street, were all decked out in "black". Black stood out as the colour of choice, as the sharp-eyed Freddy looked from street to street, heading deeper and deeper into the centre of London. There was more 'black' to be seen; black coats, black hats, black dresses, black trousers, black scarves and black gloves. Within a week, he too, was dressed in black. Freddy missed the green that was for prosperity and the gold that was for the glowing sunshine of his Caribbean homeland. Now all he had was 'black', which was for hardships in his native Caribbean country. Green, gold and black were the colours of the Jamaican flag.

It seemed to Freddy that he had symbolically lost the prosperity and sunshine and now only had the representation of hardship - "black". Therefore, when Olympics 2012 came around some years later, for him, it was a welcome reminder of home as the green and gold colours were highly visible on the streets of London, worn not only by Jamaicans but by other fans of the Jamaica track team.

In the meantime, sitting in the automobile and making his way through the city, the high buildings on either side of the streets formed the towering sides of the Grand Canyon that Freddy was now passing through. Craning his neck, he could only scope up to about five floors of these gigantic buildings, fully aware that more floors lay on top forming layers, reminiscent of a multi-layered whopper burger, with a cheese layer followed by a meat layer followed by a lettuce layer and whatever else; going up and up and up. Now on the outskirts of the city centre, the surroundings seemed more serene but the red double decker buses reminded Freddy that he was truly in London and this was no nursery rhyme.

Chapter 4

The Pink Bus Ticket

So, this was the evening of the first day – Freddy's first day of sojourn into the City of London. All the time, admiring the modern architecture of towering stone and glass structures that stood so majestically along the route, leading to his destination somewhere in the north of London; for there he would stay for a time.

His first meal on his first night consisted of potatoes. His research led him to learn as the weeks went by, that potatoes were the go-to staple for the Great British mealtime; roast, diced, sliced, mashed, wedged and jacketed. And in between main meal times, the dear potatoes would come to the table again as "crisps". And what a range of crisps to choose from; salt and vinegar, cheese and onion, smoky bacon, prawn cocktail and ready salted. Freddy needed to get used to this and fast.

He stayed awake for hours that night looking out on the starlit night of London and viewed a few planes going by, for he was still in awe of the miracle of a plane staying aloft, propelled by some thrust of aviation power. An Act of God. Hours later, Freddy took his rest.

Morning came soon after and with company, Freddy ventured out expectantly for a stroll and a ride on the red double-decker bus. He was now in receipt of his first paper bus pass. This was a semi-rigid pink card, the same size as a bank debit card or a driving licence. The norm was to purchase this pass at a local shop before boarding a bus and could be bought for a day or a month and shown to the bus driver upon entry. For this newbie in London, his sense of expectation built up as he made ready to travel into the busier parts of the city. Then came the red bus. Pink ticket held visibly for the driver to see and he was on, riding high upstairs, on the red double decker bus.

As mentioned before, Freddy had heard many stories about life in the UK told by returning friends and family, however, he was not feeling as spellbound and enraptured as the earlier migrants supposedly felt upon their arrival. This was now the Twenty-first Century and through new technology, media and higher education, Freddy was generally more prepared for life in a large modern city. He had left the Caribbean when most services and facilities that were available in London, existed in the larger Caribbean cities. Investors and entrepreneurs who had travelled to big cities abroad had returned. They established similar services to facilitate a modern-day lifestyle in the Caribbean. Thus, life in the New Millennium in Port of Spain, Bridgetown, Georgetown, Kingston, Castries and other cities, possessed attributes of any other international urban centre.

The hypnotic effect was less enthralling than anticipated, partly because Freddy was of a new generation and had been taken through hours and hours of vicarious experiences. The informal reports of the trailblazers played a significant role too, in his understanding of the social attributes of the UK. As the pioneers of five decades earlier landed upon the shores of Great Britain in 1948, from all accounts, Great Britain was a world apart from the Caribbean Islands. The wide streets, widespread use of electric power, busy roads and telephones, all seemed quite common place to Freddy and his colleagues, when they arrived in the New Millennium. They took it all in stride, as many of the facilities existed in the Islands, however, it was quite a different reality when the *Empire Windrush* arrived.

Leaving Jamaica five decades earlier, salt fish was the food of the poor and 'run-dung' and dumplin formed an important part of the culinary set up. Breddah Paul or a Maas Timothy would have been the sole motor car owner in a district. Someone of African-Caribbean descent or a family of Chinese descent ran the local shop for miles around, which was lit at nights by lanterns held on a string hung from a nail on the ceiling. And away from the parish capitals, a stone and gravel road - with the occasional asphalt – was the main surface linking rural communities, for the most part. The landline telephone was a missing feature and the mobile phone was unheard of.

As told by the first group of migrants, there were

local conflicts in the UK between those who sought to show authority within the communities and those who arrived from overseas to settle and make a living within these communities. While these conflicts between some community groups in the UK and the early Caribbean Diaspora were divisive, they created a unifying spirit among the migrants who vowed to assert their identity while living in a culture far removed from theirs.

Freddy had no personal knowledge of the *Skin Heads*, *Teddy Boys*, or the *National Front*. The ideology of such groups had become less prevalent and more latent by the time he arrived in Great Britain – the country had become more culturally tolerant by the New Millennium, as there were millions of non-ethnic nationalities living and working in the UK by that time. Consequently, there was quicker and easier assimilation into aspects of the city life, however, this many believe has to be on-going.

When Freddy arrived in Great Britain, The Thatcherite era was gone and Tony Blair had promulgated a new beginning - a new time, in principle, a new party policy - New Labour. Migration was on the rise. The EU was growing. Then came the Euro, and banana had lost its protection coming in from Jamaica. The cauldron of discontent and impatience with Saddam Hussein was bubbling and heading for over spill. The USA was only just recovering from the tragedy of 9/11. The American troops were bombing the Torah Bora hills of Afghanistan, in search of Osama Bin Laden. Britain was headed for war in Iraq. 'Weapons of Mass Destruction' were said to be in Saddam's arsenal and this worried the rest - the West. These events were a concern to many and Britain was getting ready for battle in Iraq, nay, to liberate the Iraqi people from the tyrannical leader.

These were not all gloomy, fretful and harrowing times. The spirit of London was high and the politics merely punctuated day to day life, providing media debate for those who so wished to participate. The media frenzy was frequently neutralised by the Blairite spin doctors who, sought to pacify and justify. The marches commenced on the streets of London, as the invasion of Iraq became imminent. A city of vast diversity in cultures was bound to find an outpouring of sympathy for the Middle Eastern states; given the diverse groups of Middle Eastern nationals who were living in the UK. So, when the British forces invaded Bagdad, Britain was divided. The war ended soon but the debate dragged on.

Within two years, however, another talking point would gain momentum.

"*The City of London has won the bid to host the 2012 Olympic Games,*" said the broadcaster on the radio.

Olympic fever immediately gripped the city of London and with golden boy if you will, Usain St Leo Bolt and the team of Jamaican athletes coming to town, a new kind of debate was on. This debate was taken beyond the media circle and the Olympic debate was localised and personalised. It was as though a new menu was on offer in kitchens, bars, pubs, tea houses, cafes and bistros in London. The main dish was "London 2012". Not much more was discussed.

There were doubts by some pundits that the games would succeed in London. There was discussion about the fitness of various athletes. How many medals would Team GB win? Would there be a new British sensation? And there was speculation about the budget to get things ready on time. A security speculation also arose and gained momentum over the months leading up to the games.

In all of this, there was the personal matter of the 'green' and 'gold' for Freddy.

The Olympics in London meant that the 'gold' and 'green' colours that Freddy had lost upon arrival at Heathrow, years earlier, would - though fortuitously in a way – now come back to him in London. And so was it. For the duration of the games Freddy got back the 'green' and the 'gold' that he needed to go with his attire; to go with the predominant black he was wearing in the UK, especially in the winter. With the Jamaican athletes, led by Usain Bolt and Shelly Ann Fraser-Pryce, his spirit would be lifted.

London came together following the awarding of the Olympic Games to the city, as generations, races, social classes and languages eagerly anticipated 'The Games'. However, one day later, the 7/7 bombings on the London Transport service, shifted the momentum. However, this never changed the will and desire to make London 2012 one of the best Olympic games there ever was. Freddy lived through these ups and downs and saw the transformation of Stratford from a less desirable part of the city, to becoming the home of the Olympic Games.

On a few occasions, before London won the bid and work started to make London Olympic-ready, Freddy would go down to the old site of Waterden market. In those days, the site was an open, deserted space during the week days, which was transformed into a bazaar of shops of different products on a Sunday. Cars and vans from miles around, converged on the open lot for a giant 'car boot' sale. The Waterden market was in clear view of a bus garage, where dozens of the old Routemaster buses were stationed.

*****

The formation of the Routemaster buses parked in their bays, was an iconic sight. They were being phased out but the few that remained, ran along certain routes in the city. With an open door at the rear left-hand side, passengers hopped on and off whenever it was safe to do so, without the bus coming to a halt. This was a feat that needed some skill to be performed successfully. The motion of the moving bus often-times dragged the leaving passenger forward jerkily and disembarking had to be followed by a timely trot-along until stability is regained by the body. The passenger, having disembarked successfully, would bask in the proud accomplishment of that feat for the rest of the day or at least, for the next few hours, for this was part of London city life.

*****

Standing in Waterden market on a Sunday, presented a piece of East London's social, commercial and cultural landscape. Hundreds of bargain hunters would descend on the open field opposite the bus garage each Sunday morning, in search of a bargain. This was the kind of social and commercial endeavour that characterized Great Britain and it attracted the early and later migrants who travelled to the UK. This kind of market scene was a reminder to many migrants of what they knew and lived for, before emigrating.

When London won the bid, however, the market site gave way to the construction of a New Stratford City 'Olympic Village'. A drive through the local area today bears very little similarity to what it was like before the transformation. New flats, new train station, the Olympic stadium, the aquatic centre and a new shopping centre, bear no reminders of the old days.

Chapter 5

The Barber Shop

"Whaa gwaan?" asked Rico.

"Irie," Freddy replied.

The barber shop in the New Millennium in Britain is just as important as the barber shop of the Twentieth Century. Early migrants quickly found that the barber shop was one way to re-create the communities that they left behind in the Caribbean. There was even a popular television programme of an earlier time, that used the barber shop to create a living-room-like effect and highlighted the role of the barber shop for the Diaspora in Great Britain. Arriving several years later, Freddy realised that nothing had changed from the TV series barber shop presentation, to the way he was experiencing it now.

Rico's barber shop was more than a place for a haircut. There were several ways in which the barber shop served the Diaspora. It was a football strategy room. Everyone at the barber shop knew what formation Sir Alex Ferguson should use for the Manchester United upcoming game. Everyone knew the forward line that Arsene Wenger should use in the next Arsenal game. Some said a 4-3-3 was the way forward for Arsenal, others thought it should be 5-3-2. They all had an opinion that was so fluid.

The barbers and the clients were coaches, managers, advisors and officials, all this from the comfort of the barber shop. They knew it all. They made it known to all and sundry, much to the annoyance of the clients who came for a quick haircut. A quick haircut meant enduring frequent disruptions, as one half of the hair is cut and the barber stops. He stops to join in and make his contribution about the best goalkeeper that Tottenham Hotspur should use for the home match. By now you see that a quick haircut was not something that was on the menu at Rico's. But what Rico's lacked in efficient haircuts, it made up for in atmosphere. Those unofficial team sheets and match analyses were priceless.

The barber shop had four barbers. Four fixed chairs arranged along the left-hand side leading away from the entrance. Each workspace was fitted with a cupboard kitted with the paraphernalia of the trade: shaving cream, rubbing alcohol, powder, razors, scissors, combs and towels, all arranged in some semblance of order. You could not miss the range of trimmers plugged into the extension socket close to the floor, with cords running vertically up to a makeshift trimmer holder, for easy access. Each work station had no less than four trimmers of different sizes, speeds, shapes and purposes.

The rectangular room was completed by four hair dressing stations running parallel on the right-hand side, stretching away from the entrance towards the back of the room. The centre of the room was left as a walkway and provided access to the door at the back of the room. A door in the centre of the rear wall led out into the makeshift tea room, purpose built bathroom and stock room. It was nothing short of brilliance and difficult not to admire how cleverly the small space had been used.

The hair dressers' stations were as equally functional in layout as the barbers'. As one would expect, the familiar dome-shaped device hung at the back of each chair on the right-hand side, for each hair dresser. These were for drying women's hair. A floating shelf extended along the wall serving the four hair dressing stations. A holder with spaces for curling thongs and other kinds of styling devices was at each work section, on the floating shelf. Bottles and jars of gel, creams and oils of different colours and odours sat on this shelf, adjacent to the fixed chairs.

Maggie was the head hair dresser - a very easy-going and well-liked worker in her mid-thirties. Then there was Rosie, pleasant and diligent at what she does. Sheena was quite popular and had customers of the Diaspora coming to her from all different corners of London. Jackie was fairly new, however, she commanded the respect of all who walked into that space. While they had their own conversations about what matters to girls, they were no match for the men across the shop floor. Any conversation among the women would soon be drowned out by the shouting of the men who knew everything about everything. Sport. Music. Politics. Cars.

The barbers were more than colleagues. They were a family. Their children came by. The shopping was taken there. Birthday parties were planned there. Funerals, christenings and weddings were planned at the barber shop and the extended family would form the guest list. Freddy's first experience of one such barber shop family event, was Rico's Birthday party.

"Rico party coming up, have to get some new clothes," said Reggie.

"When is the party?" Freddy asked.

"Three weeks' time but we getting tings ready," he continued.

"You waan come?" Reggie asked.

"Yea, I would love to, where him keeping it?" enquired Freddy.

"Down Waterden Road," Reggie replied.

"I don't know how to get there," said Freddy.

"Doan worry man, you can come wit me but if mi car full, you can roll wit Bobby, doan worry," he assured Freddy.

In addition to being the site of the Sunday market, before the Olympic village construction, Waterden Road had a popular venue that was frequently rented for functions. This too was later demolished to make way for the Olympic village for London 2012, much to the disappointment of Londoners who frequently rented that venue. It was this popular venue that would be used for Rico's birthday event.

Now you might see how the relationship among the barbers was that of a family, rather than colleagues and they all knew the protocol. Reggie worked in the shop and there he was informing Freddy of the birthday party and going further to place Freddy on the guest list. Rico had no knowledge that this was going on but it would not matter if Rico knew, as Reggie was part of the inner family circle. Wonder not as to Freddy's position here, as by this time he had become a part of the extended family. The extended family of Rico's barber shop included all clients and their immediate families.

By virtue of a few visits to the barber shop and routinely nodding and smiling in agreement, seldom disagreeing with the sporting analyses and voicing the odd opinion now and again, Freddy was part of the extended family.

Barnie was the third member of the barber shop male staff team. He was very reserved but had strong views on how Arsene Wenger should do his job. Needless to say, he was a die-hard Arsenal fan. He came to odds with Rico and Reggie on many occasions, as the latter two were supporters of Tottenham Hotspur.

"Barnie, when you going to support a good team?" Reggie would taunt.

"What good team, there is one good team, Arsenal, only problem is that Wenger won't listen to me and move Thierry Henry to play on the flank," Barnie would reply.

"Yuh team is history man, I goin' buy you a blue kit

this season, so you can support a good team," retorted Reggie.

This would go on for a length of time. Banter they called it. Customers who dropped by during such exchanges, would add their share of banter. You did not have to be in need of a haircut to stop by at Rico's. Some friends of the "family" would stop for as little as two minutes; they enquired how everyone was doing and were off again. They stopped by to find the whereabouts of each other too.

"Whaa gwaan, anybody see Matta?" a customer popped in to ask on one occasion, "I caan get him on the phone."

"Yes, him gone into Stratford to get some cement to do a job," someone replied.

"Aw'right, I will try him phone 'gain later," he said.

You could rest assured that someone at the barber shop would know something of the whereabouts of any of the regulars. This was a perfect example of how the barber shop functioned as a social and cultural hub. Each one was his brother's keeper. There was hardly a dull or quiet moment at Rico's.

The experience at Rico's formed the social backdrop for the Jamaican Diaspora. Freddy spent his first few months in the UK observing the communal cohesion provided by Rico's barber shop. The conclusion is that the role and function of the barber shop shows no sign of changing anytime soon. The Diaspora has maintained its uniqueness through these meeting points and they keep the home-away-from-home ideology intact.

Chapter 6

That Grammar Thing

Freddy would be drawn away into another sphere of life in the UK, during work hours, as he was teaching in one of London's most difficult secondary schools. He had been acutely aware of this professional role, as he had gained many years of experience in Jamaica. Now, he was seeing first-hand the similarities and differences between the British education system and the pedagogical framework of the Caribbean, even though the educational structure of the Caribbean is a heritage of the 'motherland' from colonial times. One of the first usage of grammar that he had to adjust to in the UK was *'different to...'*, for he was steeped in the ways of the British education legacy in the Caribbean and he could not quite embrace the use of what seemed to be a misplaced preposition but seemed to be standard usage all around.

For Freddy and his colleagues who were recruited in

the New Millennium to teach in the British schools, they would soon learn that the rudiments of teaching and learning the English grammar in the Caribbean commonwealth, was *different from* the way it was taught in schools in Great Britain.

Great Britain left the legacy for teaching grammar in the Caribbean, however, coming into Great Britain from a former colony, the recruits were amazed at the range of differences in how education was provided. Shockingly, the new recruits realised that there was no real need for a pupil in a secondary school in the UK to bring a bag into school. NO BAG? How could that be? But yes, it was possible.

Freddy especially could still hear his teacher's voice ringing in his ears, "Pack your bag from tonight, so that you don't forget your books for tomorrow."

Taking a bag to school and back home in the evenings, was how things were in the Caribbean. Students had a routine and part of that was to make sure that their bags were packed with books and equipment for the relevant subjects for the following day. Carrying a bag with books gave students in the Caribbean a sense of pride and responsibility.

Speaking of books, it was common for students in the British schools to leave their books at school in the evenings. Almost as a rule, the books were for the teacher to look after. BOOKS LEFT IN SCHOOL? One would not dare to think of it in the Caribbean. Who was going to look after them? Besides, books were needed nightly for homework, or for revision. To add to that, books were the prized possession of each student in the

Caribbean. The group of teachers arriving in the UK were from the Caribbean orientation, where parents had no such fortune of getting books delivered and given to their children for free in school.

"Whey is yuh book?" - a question almost every child would hear and fear, at some point in their school life. "*Yuh book*" was actually "your" book; with the emphasis on the possessive pronoun 'your', for each boy or girl looked after his or her own book. Students purchased their books. Hence, 'your book' meant something very personal.

Whenever the teachers met, they shared their amazement with such differences in student-school responsibility and agreed that perhaps, owning your own book added more commitment to preserving it and being accountable to parents. Freddy, for one, knew that a lot was riding on the use and preservation of 'yuh book' while growing up in the Caribbean. The education derived from the ownership, use and preservation of books, was a route for social mobility and the best effort was needed at the first academic opportunity, as there were no free second chances. Every hour of academic learning came at a premium price.

*****

Now Freddy had his first job in, to say the least, a challenging school in the East End of London. He walked in on his first morning, in time for staff briefing.

From there he met with the Human Resources person, who sorted out his timetable and a few other bits of initial inventory formalities. Freddy met his first class for the day and as expected, there were a few questions related to "setting the ground rules". He anticipated the first question, as he was fully aware that his students would be keen to know about his ethnicity.

"Sir, where're you from?" asked Billy.

"Jamaica," Freddy confidently replied.

It was Freddy's guess that the following question would be an inquisition into his status, age, travel history, favourite sport or some such query as may occupy the minds of students trying to figure out the make, model and specifications of a new teacher.

"Sir, do you smoke weed?" Billy continued.

"No, why did you ask me that?" Freddy asked.

"Sir, every Jamaican smoke weed," Billy assured him.

Freddy's astonishment was palpable, as the student proceeded to explain his source of information.

"I know some Jamaicans round my way sir, and they smoke weed."

Bizarrely, the survey and hence the conclusion of the student was based on a sample size of the few Jamaicans 'round his way' - a conclusion that was hardly empirical. Realising the small sample size of Jamaicans in the student's research, Freddy tried to negate the student's findings and to dispel the stereotype that he had about Jamaicans. Freddy concluded, however, that the stereotyping was embedded in a fashion, akin to the mental coding undergone by special agents to protect their mission, and no simple interrogation would blow that cover.

Whether Billy was convinced that as a Jamaican by birth, Freddy would have a better idea or him as a non-Jamaican, with the knowledge of a few people 'round his way' would know better, remained unknown. It was unclear to Freddy why anyone would choose to uphold rumours and stereotypes instead of learning the truth from a trustworthy source. Knowing and accepting the truth might bring about a shift in a deep-rooted mental paradigm; a shift that may be too painful to process and accept sometimes.

*****

The first day expectations of the teaching role, were something of an amazement for Freddy, as he was required to begin by handing out free exercise books from one of the several boxes that he was given to distribute in his classes. The books were colour coded for each department and blue was the colour for Freddy's subject department. Now mesmerised, Freddy then followed up the book distribution with the pen distribution, as pens were also handed out as a part of the national provision for students in Great Britain. After repeating the process five times for that day, "sir" had fulfilled his duties, by ensuring that all his learners had their vital equipment - book and pen.

The experience of working and living in the East End

of London can be a cultural awareness exercise, as much as it can be educational. The diverse ethnic mix in this part of London provides a view into some of the more exotic cultures, particularly from the Asian countries. A large Bangladeshi, Pakistani, Indian and to a lesser extent, Sri Lankan Diaspora, occupy many of the communities in the East End of London. As a cricket fanatic, Freddy could appreciate the excitement for the game all around him; an excitement which found its way into the school where he worked.

Freddy was to find out some years later that cricket was a main sport only in London schools with large Asian populations. It was a rare sight to see a boy or girl going to school with a cricket bat in boroughs such as Haringey, Hackney, Southwark or Camden. Football was the main focus in these and many other London boroughs. Say "football" in most London schools and you had everyone's attention.

Inside the schools, lessons in the UK had to be differentiated, so that learning material must be of varying degrees of difficulty and varying styles of content. This is to ensure that the various ability and learning needs are targeted. Not only was the teacher required to plan the lessons but each lesson in principle, had two to three sub lessons; each targeting the different ability levels per class. The custom in the Caribbean was to group students in classes according to their ability levels. The teacher therefore, did not have to make as many sub-lessons. This made planning more focused on students of similar ability...and it worked. It worked well.

Freddy's initiation in the East End was the backdrop to an educational, social, cultural and meteorological introduction to Great Britain. As he recalls from his research, the weather in the UK was unstable and several atmospheric conditions could present themselves within a short period of time, so that up to four distinct weather features could occur within an hour or two. The winter months soon came on and this gave Freddy a sublime lesson in meteorology, London style.

Chapter 7

Snow Misery

Winter. By this time, winter was in full flow. It was January and still no sign of the white, flakey substance. Before journeying to the UK, Freddy and his colleagues read about the joys of beholding that white, flakey substance. A Christmas card sent back from the Jamaican Diaspora would invariably show a house with snow-covered roof and trees, with icicles hanging like stalactites from the leaves and branches.

These cards, over the years made family and friends in the Caribbean form an opinion that England was forever under snow. It was not the reality but somehow, that was the conclusion. Did you ever see a post card from Great Britain depicting a hot summer day with skimpily clad Britons, basking in the sun in Hyde Park? How about a postcard with Britons sweating in the sun in South-End-on-Sea? NEVER. How about a postcard with topless male drinkers by the pub? Not in any one's memory who lived in the Caribbean. And what of a postcard showing a barbeque in thirty-five-degree Celsius sunshine, with chicken and sausages sizzling on the grill in someone's back garden?

Never were such depictions of Great Britain displayed on a postcard or Christmas card, sent from relatives and friends who resided in Great Britain. And owing to this one-sided depiction of Great Britain, the Islanders conjured up an inevitability of England's annual 'white Christmas', yet this 'white Christmas' was rare.

*****

Freddy was at home on the evening of January 30, 2003, when the snow came. It came abundantly and mercilessly. Within an hour, there was no sighting of the streets anymore, just the white, even, crisp carpet that obscured all that lay close to the ground.

Children and adults alike needed no invitation to be outside in gardens and driveways, making merry. The snow seemed to be a welcome inconvenience, as access to shops and services was curtailed. A snowball here and a snowman there, spoke of the light-hearted spirit enkindled by this cushion of flakey precipitation blanketing the ground. However, while most Britons enjoyed the sudden cascading of snow, there was agony and misery for others. Across the UK, commuters were trapped in their vehicles on roads that had become impassable.

The updates online and news broadcasts on TV, were sobering to an otherwise frenzied and euphoric response to the snow.

One news headline was: *"Thousands trapped in snow storm."*

This was almost a paradox as the snow was perceived as a providence of joy, solace, tranquillity, peace and goodwill to all men - and women. The children and adults who were playing and making snow men - and women, were worlds apart from the misery of adults and children marooned in their vehicles on the roads.

The contrast and severe reality of the effect of the snow was coming closer to home, as the new Londoners listened to the broadcasts.

A later news report stated: *"Motorists still facing snowy misery."*

"Some oxymoron this was," thought Freddy. 'Snow misery'. This juxtaposition contrasts joy and sorrow. The 'joy' was flaunted by those gambolling in the snow and only the suffering thousands trapped on the roads, could understand the 'misery' brought on by the snow.

"Snow brings chaos to London," another report stated.

These sobering reports tempered the frivolity of snow games. Thousands were hungry, cold and in need of toilet facilities but were rendered immobile by the snow, not knowing when they would get to a comfortable place. Most discomforting was news of a bus transporting disabled passengers, that was trapped on the Motorway, amidst the traffic.

Hearing of such obvious desperation, made Freddy reflect upon his own past misery. A misery he had endured during a hurricane. Hurricane, as a rule, is not a phenomenon that affects England, although there have been unexpected hurricanes. A devastating hurricane named *Gilbert*, made its appearance onto the Jamaican mainland, in 1988. The consequences were deadly. As Freddy's memory went back to his *Gilbert* encounter, he shared absolute empathy with the commuters trapped in the snow blitz on the roadways, in the UK. He was trapped on the roadway in Jamaica, during the onslaught of the violent hurricane *Gilbert*.

*****

Just barely out of Sixth form, Freddy had taken his first job with the Ministry of Social Security. He travelled a total of seventy-four miles return to work each day, by public transport. That is some distance to travel for work, however, at the time, he relished the hours spent travelling. The longer the travelling time, the longer time to listen to a range of reggae beats in the minibuses, for at the time, minibus operators were allowed to play a choice of reggae music, in their public passenger vehicle.

Having listened to the weather bulletin on the Sunday evening, everyone knew that the hurricane was coming the next day. Foolishly, Freddy set out on his thirty-seven-mile journey to work.

"I doan think you should leave the house today, this hurricane is serious you kno," his father cautioned.
Older and wiser - he had seen a few devastating hurricanes over the years.

"It is a category four hurricane, it will be dangerous," his mother added.
She knew that there was no safety outside for anyone, during a hurricane.

Youthful exuberance, supposedly, got in the way and off to work Freddy went, ignoring his parents' caution. He left home for work that bleak Monday morning, under a cloud of certainty – a certainty that the storm was nigh. A certainty that there would be damage, destruction and devastation.

His family never heard from him again until late Wednesday afternoon; some 56 hours later.

His nightmare started pretty much the way it started for the people trapped in their vehicles along the roads, during the snow in the UK. Freddy had made it into work but all the signs were clear that the hurricane was swiftly approaching the Island. A moderate breeze started, as he left the office by mid-day on that Monday. His manager, sensing the imminent peril, had made it clear that all staff should leave and head back home without delay.

"The hurricane has just hit Kingston and it is coming this way fast," he had said.

"I am closing the office, so you can all get home quickly," the manager concluded.

With some knowledge of the physical geography of the Caribbean Islands and Jamaica in particular, it is easy to understand why Freddy and his colleagues could be at work while the winds raged in Kingston. The hurricane winds usually move in a Westerly or West-North-Westerly direction, from the Atlantic Ocean towards the Greater Antilles and Central America. This means that the Eastern parishes were hit first by the winds. Their office was in the West.

With all the workers being gently persuaded out of the office by the manager, Freddy managed to make it to the first change- over point on the journey home, when the streets around him became deserted. Taxis and buses had stopped running. Trees were all swaying and galvanised roofing was starting to come away from roofs on the buildings around him. The shops were just turning out the last of the desperate shoppers, who had descended upon the shops for emergency supplies of rice, batteries, lanterns, matches, bread and canned meats.

Freddy quickly grabbed what was left on the shelf of the last shop that was open, in the little town of Hopewell. What was left were two packs of rock cakes; each pack containing two cakes. This meant he had a grand total of four rock cakes to keep him through the hurricane. Now, fully prepared for a night on the street with his four rock cakes, he was less than ceremoniously ejected from the shop, as the owner pulled the shutter down, narrowly missing his heels. Freddy was now on the shop porch, with the storm for company.

The streets around him were now empty. Plastic cups and bits of paper were being pushed like flotsam and jetsam upon waves, bobbing here and there across the road. Clearly, this was '*Gilbert*'. Hurricane Gilbert was in full fury. The last motor car in the town square disappeared around the bend. So, there he stood. One man, equipped with four rock cakes, to face the storm.

By divine intervention, Freddy remembered that a colleague lived a stone's throw from the shops on the high road, in that community of Hopewell. In one desperate dash, he made off, rock cake in hand, crossed the road, ran up the adjacent hill, went around the bend, over the ditch, through the gates and onto her veranda, to seek refuge from what was now a raging storm. Another family had turned up there for refuge too.

Forty-eight hours later, they would have survived with two hours' sleep on a wet bed, three flooded rooms, two broken glass windows, a partly missing roof and bandaged feet from cuts received from broken glass. The trepidation of a large ackee tree falling directly onto the window of the front room; smashing the panes of glass to smithereens, still lingers in Freddy's memory.

With electricity disconnected for health and safety reasons and water supplies turned off, to prevent unwanted flooding, Freddy, the other sheltered family and the hosts, had to survive on emergency food. From a roasted breadfruit plucked from the fridge and two tins of sardines, they had their first meal the next morning. With the remaining portion of sardines and the rock cakes, they had another meal on Tuesday afternoon.

The hurricane had passed and in its wake, a narrative of destruction was left: severed roads, disrupted water supply, uprooted trees, missing houses, roofless buildings, bare hillsides and widespread misery. 'Misery' which is a reminder of the snow in London.

*****

The trapped commuters on the motorway in the UK eventually got to complete their journey; albeit very late on that night of January 30, 2003. They made it home belatedly to warm beds and supposedly a *cuppa*. By the following day, the snowmen had melted and all that remained where they stood, were the coins used for eyes and the carrots that substituted as noses.

Chapter 8

Miss Johnson and Katie

One of the profound differences that exists between the early Diaspora and the migrants who arrived at the start of the New Millennium, is the position of scholarly responsibility that was entrusted to the latter. The Caribbean had limited opportunities for academic pursuits, when the early migrants set sail for Great Britain in the 1940s. By the time the New Millennium started, Great Britain was looking to the independent Jamaica for qualified teachers.

Jamaica to the rescue - again. This time, the pivotal and delicate responsibility was to educate the next generation of British children. Jamaicans were now asked to educate English nationals in the *motherland*. While Miss Lou, a famous Jamaican writer, had penned her poem, *"Colonisation in Reverse"*, years earlier, there was now more merit given to her comedic poem.

In her poem, Miss Lou alluded to the 'colonisation'

of the Caribbean Islands in the Seventeenth Century, by the British. As Caribbean nationals were sailing away to Great Britain in the Twentieth Century, she made reference to the irony of the Islanders going now to seemingly 'colonise' Britain.

Teacher Freddy and his colleagues were now in the UK, as they fit the criteria of being passionate, confident and tenacious.

A colleague who arrived with Freddy, explained a gripping conversation that she had during the morning break in her school, when a student walked into her classroom. They had never met before, as that student was not on her timetable. The conversation, she told Freddy, began with the student asking, "Miss, where are you from?" This question would have been asked a thousand times, by curious students who were now being taught by a new set of teachers from Jamaica. For them, this was an unusual phenomenon.

"Jamaica," she replied.

"What's your name Miss?" the student continued.

"Miss Johnson," said the teacher. "And what's your name?" the teacher asked.

"Katie," the student replied.

"Miss Johnson, what do you teach?" the student asked.

"English," replied Miss Johnson.

"What!" Katie exclaimed. "A Jamaican in England teaching English?" "Wow!" she concluded.

Miss Johnson and Katie continued the conversation for the rest of the break. Katie was overawed by the reality that was revealed there and then. The student's response was quite uplifting and reassured Miss Johnson of her profile in the new British pedagogical structure.

Miss Johnson had never stopped to make much ado about her job. It was her profession and she just carried on with her job to get the best out of her students. Katie's remark and the ensuing conversation, says much about 'Post- Independence' Jamaica. Miss Johnson was now quite 'chuffed', as is said in Great Britain. On each of her bad days, she would be buoyed by the memory of that conversation with Katie.

There were many others like Miss Johnson. She, like others who arrived at the dawn of the New Millennium, could now provide more accurate descriptions of Great Britain for colleagues back in the Caribbean. Other teachers wanted to follow. The mobile phone and the internet in 2000, made communication fast and immediate. There was no waiting around, as in the case of the *Empire Windrush* generation, for updates. Where visual proof and illustrations were required, a mobile phone could easily capture real-time images, to be sent Worldwide.

This was a new exodus that was set in motion in 2000. The exodus gathered momentum in 2001. It grew in 2002. By 2003, it had dwindled and agencies recruited far less numbers than before, as a result of government legislature. Nevertheless, recruitment has continued, as these educators have been an indisputable proof of the academic opulence of the Caribbean in general and Jamaica, in particular.

However, the extent to which the story has been told

is still not known. Their brilliance may have upstaged some of the long-standing views and stereotypes of Jamaicans. Here was now a new perspective of the achievements of the Island, a new advertisement and a new reality being presented internationally as a show-piece to the world. The Canadian and American schools also benefitted from the expertise of these educators, when North American agencies followed the British agencies into Jamaica.

Chapter 9

Dean's Promotion

The tales of Freddy and his contemporaries who arrived in the UK, are phenomenal and in just a few months after arriving, their achievements tell of their brilliance. Dean's promotion came as a result of his dedication and outstanding work, at his school in the East End of London. Carol and Dave are two others who also made a noteworthy contribution to the development of academic pedagogy in their schools.

Freddy and Dean had arrived just as the Summer months were ending. For them, seventeen degrees Celsius was cold but a blanket of air measuring just that, was descending upon London by the time the school year had started. Twenty-five degrees in the Caribbean was a cold day - warm jumpers, woolly hats and thick trousers would come to everyone's rescue. This was now sheer agony for these two Caribbean friends, who needed to adjust fast to the autumn weather. All those layers of under and outer clothing they now wore in the UK, did little to bring back the thirty degrees they had left behind. Needless to say, they spent many hours brooding and lamenting the decision to migrate to Great Britain.

By coincidence or providence, Freddy and Dean were placed in the same school, in the East End of London. Dean taught Geography. Freddy would spend a few minutes in the morning, checking up on Dean to find out how things were going in his lessons. It was not uncommon to hear how many paper planes were confiscated, how many instances of swearing there were, how many pens had the ink deliberately leaked out - those pens again! The same pens that had to be routinely handed out.

Spare a thought for the teacher who, having handed out pens and books on one day to ask on the next day, "Where is your pen?" And the response is, "It has no ink."

It was pointless for the teacher to give a reminder such as: "But I gave you a new pen yesterday."

That would be followed by something similar or close to: "I didn't do anything, I swear down, the ink just leaked out." Or "Yea, but look it's not working now, the ink is gone."

Whenever Dean relayed a tale of empty pens, it made no headlines, as the story re-occurred on many days. Freddy had similar horror stories too and would relate stories of how new exercise books would be finished after three days. And the reason for this can be summed up in two words - paper planes.

There would be times, however, when Dean would relay other stories about the student who finished all the work and completed additional tasks. There was very little variation in the day to day tales and rules and sanctions remained the same.

The classrooms were much calmer in the Caribbean and there was a keen sense of competition amongst the students. There was, by and large, a desire to succeed. This made a sharp contrast for Freddy and his colleagues in the British classrooms, where protests were stunningly normalised. Most instructions given by the teachers were met with questions.

"Is it just me?" "Did you see me do it?" "Why?" "What about him?" These questions followed many instructions that were given to students. Many valuable hours of learning time were lost in responding to such questions, which were usually asked as an orchestrated means of delaying the pedagogical process. The Caribbean teachers soon realised that, in these instances of orchestrated time wasting, no one complained. Other students waited for however long it took for the work to get back on track, with muted indifference. As relayed by Dean, he had willed himself to reality a few times, as he found it surprising that there was usually little show of annoyance amongst peers in the lessons, to these time-wasting methods. Such methods would have been frowned upon by the classmates, in Caribbean schools.

Then there were things like playground break duty to be done, and sometimes, school 'gate duty' and 'corridor duty'. The classroom itself, was a constant duty - on the lookout for things like bullying and truancy, listening out for offensive words and swearing.

Freddy and Dean, like many others who arrived in the New Millennium, did well despite the contrasting workplace scenarios and were acknowledged by their British managers. Within two years, Dean was given a promotion, which came as some shock to him. Mr John Hollingsfield, the Head teacher, walked into his classroom one morning before lesson had begun. As was customary, Freddy would be in Dean's classroom before work started in the morning. Mr Hollingsfield therefore, found them both preparing for the day in Dean's classroom. He engaged them in a bit of casual chat about football and how they felt about certain players in the English Premier League. Like two chided schoolboys, Freddy and Dean were in fear of giving 'wrong' answers, lest they upset the fervent Manchester United supporter. Football was a religion. There was hardly a member of staff, women included, who did not support a football team.

"Colin will go on retirement leave at the end of the term and I want you to be Assistant Head of Geography, come September," said Mr Hollingsfield to Dean.
Dean, who was sitting on a stool near a cupboard, at the far end of his classroom, seemed to go pale.

"What did you say?" Dean asked, in obvious panic.
John was not the kind of man to take no for an answer. Whether he heard Dean's question, or he simply chose to ignore it, no one will ever know but he just carried on.

"If you come to me after school, I will talk you

through some of the things you will have to do and about your new salary," continued John, with Dean still in a daze.

"You are now in management, congratulations," John said.

Before Dean could recover, Mr Hollingsfield was out the door. All that the two friends could hear was the cluck, clack, cluck, clack of his shoes, making contact with the concrete flooring; fading in a decrescendo, as he disappeared down the corridor towards his office.

The overwhelmed Dean slowly recovered from the shock of his new appointment. Freddy congratulated him and left for his duty, as duties were an overarching part of their contract.

Freddy also arrived in England with a teacher, named Carol. She taught Mathematics in a large secondary school in another part of London. Despite no previous management experience, Carol was asked to be second in charge of Maths, in a department of nine full-time and two part-time teachers. This was achieved in the second year of her London experience.

Freddy and Dave, another teacher, met at a recruitment fair in Kingston, so when they ran into each other again, nearly three years later at an educational workshop in London, Dave also had his own story to share. Dave had gained the admiration of his colleagues, in the English department at his school. In his third year, he was offered the role of Deputy Head of English. For various reasons, which he later shared with Freddy, he wistfully declined, much to the dismay and annoyance of the Head teacher. Although considered to be good at his job, Dave felt that his true calling may not have been teaching and he believed that such a role in leadership may best suit a different candidate, someone who wished to deepen their tutelage within the discipline. Dave knew the job well, he had the knowledge, the skills and all the professional attributes, however, he longed to do something that made him truly happy. Freddy later learned that Dave had begun to dabble in writing and had published his first book.

Dean, Carol and Dave and many others like them, quickly stood out as the shining lights they were. These were the products of Jamaica - born, bred and educated in Jamaica. Their efficiency in carrying out their role in Great Britain raised many questions and baffled many minds. This was mainly because the Island had become synonymous with the term "yardie gangs" – a connotation of drugs and lawlessness. When these educators arrived in Great Britain from the Island of the so-called "yardie gangs", some of the connotations from an earlier decade were now at odds with the new reality, as this side of Jamaica was hitherto unknown.

Chapter 10

And there was lamb

London is a cultural melting pot. The East End is a conglomeration of cultures, with the various Asian groups being the most predominant. There are also the various African ethnic groups, who have perpetuated their social and cultural identity in the East End of London.

Most of the teachers recruited from Jamaica had been working in boroughs in the East of London. Freddy was there and found himself in the midst of the various cultural enclaves. It was on one of his exploratory walks along the high road outside Forest Gate station, that Freddy decided to venture into a function room. There was a large open area with seats arranged at the sides and small tables in front of each seating area. The small tables were used for resting of glasses, bottles, plates and whatever else the patrons may use on their evening-out.

The room was complete with two pool tables in the centre and a bar area for serving drinks, towards the left of the room upon entering. Freddy soon realised that the spoken language was African in origin and it was spoken quite loudly. He walked over to one of the pool tables to watch a game that was in progress. He must have seemed out of place as someone asked, "Are you ok my friend?"

Freddy looked behind him after hearing the question but as no one was standing behind him, he guessed that the question was for him.

"Yes, I am fine," Freddy replied after composing himself.

A few friendly smiles were made. He read that to mean that he was welcome. He was right.

There had been stories from the early Caribbean migrants about their social life in the UK. For most, it has been confined to settings where all were from the same Island. The order of their day was 'bonding with your own' but Freddy had chanced to take a wider view of that perception. Britain had been changing and the reality was that Great Britain was becoming a more culturally eclectic place. Different nationalities could exist, without any open show of hostility and where possible, mingle in social exchanges.

On this occasion, Freddy found himself in a function room surrounded by other migrants of a different cultural and ethnic orientation.

"You seem to be new around here?" the person continued.

"Yea, I just decided to come in and see what's going

on," Freddy told him.

"Oh, you are welcome anytime, we are here every Tuesday. My name is Charles."

Freddy then introduced himself. Taking the friendly welcome as his queue, Freddy carried on.

"I am new around here, so just trying to get to know the place and to familiarize myself with the events in the East End."

"Oh, I see; we are here every Tuesday night. It's our East African meeting spot," said Charles.

The conversation was going apace and so was the game of pool. The little group was now joined by Emmanuel, Solomon and Edo. Freddy soon found out that they were Ugandans and Kenyans, who shared that space. This was for them, what the barber shop was for the Jamaican Diaspora.

The two players had finished their game of pool, when Freddy was politely asked if he wished to play a set with the winner. He did not think about that too hard, before he agreed. What was not known then, was how his skills at the game would fare against the reigning champion of the moment. Dea was his name. Dea had won the last game and he was inviting the newbie to have a game with him. He must have assumed that Freddy had some knowledge or experience of the game. Dea was right in that assumption but what he, nor anyone else knew, was that Freddy's knowledge and experience had some depth. Freddy was introduced to the game in high school and after years of practice, he had become a bit of a marksman. The shot with the cue behind the back, the delicate jab to dislodge one ball without disturbing another, the long-range strike, and sinking off the bank, were all part of Freddy's repertoire.

It was game on between himself and Dea and Freddy was feeling quite at home. This was England, London in the Twenty-first Century. However, at that moment he was reminded that he was not exactly of the predominant cultural persuasion in the room. How so suddenly? Martha, the waitress, had just brought out a platter with cooked meat. She laid it on a table next to the area with the largest group of patrons. They seemed quite expectant. It was part of the custom that the host of the event provided something as a token of appreciation for their custom. Furthermore, it was a symbol of the African hospitality.

"C'mon, have some, it's good," said Solomon, willing Freddy to partake.

He enquired about the kind of meat that was on offer, as he was acutely aware that some meats eaten within some cultures might not be considered with the same merit as a Jamaican culinary delight. That kind of difference occurs even amongst the Islands of the Caribbean, despite the relatively small size of the region.

After migrating to the UK, Freddy discovered from some Guyanese friends that the iconic 'ackee', which is the national dish of Jamaica, is frowned upon in Guyana. The ackee is a symbol of unwelcome spirits and it is left to grow wild in the Guyanese jungles. The flying fish, which is a popular dish of Barbados, is considered to be poisonous and does not find its way onto the Jamaican restaurant menu, let alone into the domestic cuisine.

"Lamb. Lamb it is. Try it, it's very good, try it," Solomon replied.

With that clarification from Solomon, Freddy decided in the spirit of integration and eclectic acculturation, that he would try it. He helped himself to a piece of the lamb. This, of course, after searching around on the platter for a relatively small piece, in case he did not like it, there would be less of it to endure. For the moment, he felt somewhat integrated.

Before he left the function room, two sets of pool later and a piece of lamb devoured, Freddy was asked about his country of origin, as you might expect.

"No, no, you not from Jamaica," was the response that he got after declaring his country of origin.

He confirmed his ethnicity once more, to be given the same response. Freddy was not altogether shocked by the response, which seemed to be the general consensus of those who were involved in the conversation.

While deliberating on their reaction, he had a flashback to the conclusion that the student had arrived at in that earlier encounter at work. These friends in the function room had their own conclusions.

"Why do you say that?" Freddy asked the chief proponent of the disagreement.

"No, no, Jamaicans not like you. You too quiet to be Jamaican."

Freddy tried to set the record straight once again. Whether they were convinced or not, he would never know as a few weeks later, he went back to see his new

East African friends but the venue was: 'Sold - under new management' and the Diaspora forum had moved elsewhere.

Chapter 11

The Queen's Market

The vibrancy of the East End of London was evident in commerce and artistic presentations but one component that stood out for Freddy and his colleagues, was the commercial re-creation of the East Indies. A trip along Green Street was an undeniable reminder of the bazaars of the Punjabi region, or a New Delhi commercial centre in India. Freddy was pulled in to this spectacle by his curiosity. A curiosity that sprung up years earlier from the literature he read of the Asian traders and their thrift and enterprise. A little went a long way amongst the poorest within those Asian communities, where people looked after one another - from Peshawar, to Rawalpindi to Mumbai and Kolkata.

Freddy looked forward to going to Queen's Market, in East Ham, on a Saturday morning. On one visit to East Ham, he was shown the West Ham football stadium.

*****

For the sake of clarity, West Ham stadium is not in West Ham but actually, in East Ham; a point of confusion for many football fans. While on the subject of misplaced names - White Hart Lane stadium is not on White Hart Lane. White Hart Lane stadium is to be found on Tottenham high road - about half a mile away from White Hart Lane, adding to the confusion for football fans and visitors to Tottenham and East Ham.

*****

The journey that Freddy took from his home on a Saturday, along Green Street to Queen's Market, was fascinating as much as it was enlightening. The length of Green street was populated by shops owned or operated by someone of an Asian heritage. Asian families he guessed, occupied about ninety percent of houses along that road. A set of houses lining Green Street was intermittently punctuated by a shop of one kind or another. At an early morning hour, the local car wash would be already opened; buckets with water and grease-removing chemicals at the ready, for whichever car ventured in first. The workers, with that look of readiness and anticipation of a fair day's trade stood around, hands in pockets while all the time, screening each passing car; hoping that the next unfortunate dirty automobile was pulling in to be washed.

Further along, it was common to see shutters going up on the off-licence shops. The whirring of the pulleys operating the metal shutter was an indication that day light had arrived; it was another day and another pound to be made, if you were the owner, another pound to be spent if you were a shopper. Shutters were now pushed up, glass sliding doors pushed aside and the business day was alive. The outside stalls would soon be set up in front of the off-licence shops. A selection of vegetables, fruits and ground provisions made up the goods for sale on those stalls. Freddy lost count of the number of those off-licence shops trading along Green Street. They had one thing in common, they were operated by a member of the Asian community.

Move onwards and the smell of the chicken, panini and onion bhaji made a presence. The local cafes, for there were plenty of them, had to be early off the blocks for the day's trading. A peep inside any of the cafes exposed the rows of small tables with fours chairs, each with a plastic floral or striped table cover. On top of each table perched a jar or two of some spice; salt included and pepper. A small transparent vase with a stem or two of artificial flowers stood in company of the spice containers on each table. The cutleries were arranged at the four ends of the table, invariably bound inside a napkin.

Then there were the businesses that did not depend too heavily on first light, to start their trading. A few second-hand furniture shops, money remittances, clothes stores and travel services would still be shut in the early hours, as Freddy went by. Freddy was well and truly into Asian territory and enjoying it all. No surprises then that he was in for another phase of enlightenment, when he walked into Queen's Market at the far end of Green Street. The shoppers were dressed in saris, salwar kameez, colourful bangles, turbans, baggy trousers and sandals. There were shoppers both with children and without. The market provided a cohesion for the Asian community. Bangladeshi, Pakistani, Indians and Sri Lankans made up the bulk of the customers therein. Shrewd bargain hunters all over the world arrive at their local markets at first light and in the East End at Queen's Market, it is no different.

The spirit of the traders was always high. Mixed in amongst the Asian traders were English traders, usually dealing in meats, eggs and haberdashery items. Though in competition for the shoppers' custom, each seller seemed to have his fair share of regulars, as there were those customers who walked hastily to particular stalls. Punjabi tunes played from small music systems strung up across some stalls, creating a diegetic effect for the market day, cinematographic spectacle. The world of faraway Asian communities was being re-enacted, a space, a market, an arcade, a bazaar of some thousands of miles away. It was right there in front of Freddy - in Queen's Market. The hubbub of sounds, voice and music had him fully immersed into the fervour and life of this new cultural panorama. In time, he would make sense of the noises.

The indecipherable noises would soon start to make sense to Freddy's *foreign ears.*

"Aaaany one you choose, come over heere get all yer ripe fruits juuust one poun' da box!" bellowed one seller. Caught up in Queen's Market in the East End of London and listening to the vendors, Freddy had to wake himself. He was actually in the reality of what was merely images - images formed in his mind from films and literature, decades earlier.

"Over here sir, buying some fruits?" a vendor asked Freddy.

The voices drowned each other out. There were grapes, oranges, watermelons, avocados and apples in abundance.

"Aaaany one you choose, come over heere get all yer ripe fruits juuust wuaaan poun' da box!" repeated the previous seller. He must have repeated that line a hundred times or more each day.

There were other agricultural products. There were handmade items. The market had most things that anyone would need for a household to meet domestic living, for the coming week. The shopping suited many, as small pieces of home comforts could be bought therein. Some small tables, stools, garden tools, fans, irons, electrical extension cords and battery-operated gadgets could be picked up, however, the price was not usually fixed. Haggle and you could save yourself a penny or two.

The sellers are one half of the extravaganza and they stand ready to make a profit. The shoppers are the other half and they are in search of a bargain. The market though, seems to go beyond a selling and buying portal. There was ease and identity and a way of life. A way of life that would not be complete without the symbols of the East Indies. The range of household decorations was wide. Stretch your imagination: vases, monuments, flower pots, porcelain bowls, oriental and Asian-style lamps and it was not long until Freddy saw a carpet seller. The carpets had intricate designs and multilayers of colours, skilfully woven to form shapes of animals, buildings and some somewhat abstract patterns. Perhaps, there was more underlying the designs that Freddy considered abstract but he would never know the meanings, as he had but a limited knowledge of Asian culture and its religious renaissance.

As the weeks went by, Freddy got used to the scene. The sights and sounds of Queen's Market were so indelibly etched in his mind, that he genuinely looked forward to each and every visit on a Saturday.

Chapter 12

Of Crowds and Birds

Saturdays were full with things to do and see. The open forecourt of Stratford Station was Freddy's local recline. Long before the Olympic Games came to London, this not-so-popular city kept on buzzing with day to day activities and diverse ethnicities. A few hours spent outside the station which formed the hub of travel interchanges, could provide an education in sociology, anthropology and rare entertainment for an observer. Perched on a stool upstairs in a local eatery, across the road from the station, is where Freddy would usually sit. Most times, savouring the taste of a sandwich, while allowing the range of impressive tableaux to enlighten his eyes.

Sitting there in the eatery, he often wondered how the passengers alighting from their travel, avoided collision with the passengers going across the forecourt into the station, as they moved at quick pace from train, to bus, to tubes and to shops. The speed and accuracy of the movements of the commuters, as they went about their business, without collision, took Freddy's mind back to what he had seen a few months earlier, in the town of Brighton. This Southwestern seafront of England is better known for its beaches and events, than for its birds but Freddy beheld one of the greatest spectacles of nature in all its glory, right there at the pier in Brighton.

The pier was a bustling arena of sights, sounds, smells, trading, laughter, fright, excitement, eagerness and tired legs, all combining in that one 500-metre long structure, that extends like a turret from the shoreline. Oblivious to what was happening in the air above him, Freddy walked along the pier, when suddenly onlookers drew his attention to an exhibition above the pier. He noticed that most of the transfixed onlookers were seeking out vantage points, to gain full view of whatever it was that caught their attention.

"What are they looking at?" Freddy asked a stranger.

"Wait, wait, you will soon see," she said, without once looking at the mystified Freddy.

"They went that way," she continued while waving one hand in the direction of what used to be the other pier, which was now burnt out and rendered useless. "They will come back around any minute now," she assured Freddy.

None of her antics were helping, as Freddy remained in his misery, being no wiser about what was going on.

"Look! Look!" she screamed, with utmost excitement.

From the left of his vision, there was the most majestic pattern of flying birds that Freddy had ever seen. A flock of supposedly 2000 - 3000 birds, flew at lightning speed above and around the pier. They broke off into four smaller groups at intervals and moved away in four directions at high speed, then circled back together to form one group. They bobbed and weaved then broke off into about eight smaller groups, that criss-crossed each other, while moving upwards and sideways at high speed. The patterns were absolutely breath-taking, as the birds would continually come together and then break off into different size groups.

Could the birds count to four?

How did they know that it was time to make four groups?

And how could they know when they had five smaller groups?

Who gave the command as to which direction each group would veer off towards?

Who agreed the length of time each team would do their group manoeuvre?

Who did the countdown in each group for them to return to form the big group?

They kept this up for what seemed to be an eternity. The choreography was sensational. There was no collision among them. It was breath-takingly awesome.

*****

Sitting and watching the commuters moving and

intertwining as they hurried to and from the station on the Stratford forecourt, was a reminder for Freddy. A reminder of the bobbing and weaving of the birds on that Southwestern seafront town of Brighton. He concluded, however, that the birds' movement may have beaten the movement of the humans by way of speed, coordination and patterns – a conclusion that the humans might disagree with.

The Stratford underground was constantly busy, with people pouring out of its gates incessantly. They moved across swiftly to get onto one of the many buses that wait in the bays adjacent to the train station. The popularity of Stratford city has grown ever since and so has the flow of commuters on that forecourt.

Chapter 13

Bournemouth

It was in Bournemouth where Freddy first experienced a float parade. Having got into town quite early and venturing out to explore in the afternoon, he was just in time to see the sculptured heads of horses and dragons being carried along by revellers, accompanied by music and dance. Of course, streets were closed as was the norm in all towns that stage the time-honoured tradition of float parades. Less than two hundred metres to the south side of the main attractions, another hundred or more visitors could be seen making merry with their favourite drinks, while watching the ebb and flow of the sea. The cafe-lined beach was a frenzied back drop to the summertime merriment.

The air was heavy with the smell of burnt meats from the seaside huts, as family and friends made good of their day out for a barbeque. Some families, having added too much coal to their grill, ended up with charred meat. The commingled noises of children and their parents who traversed the pebble-strewn beach, was undoubtedly a reminder that summer was truly on. As expected, the sea side cafés sold the local favourite, cod and chips, scampi and chips and plaice and chips. Freddy tried some of the food and could see why the sea-food dishes are so popular across the country. As he tasted it, his tongue was hit by the taste of vinegar, working its way into the taste buds while all the time awakening the glands to send a sour, yet flavourful, tangy, tasty sensation upwards in his mouth towards the ears, creating a stunningly delightful effect. Odd to think that ordinary vinegar can have that fibrillating effect on the human taste buds.

The food, drinks and games provided the excitement. The excitement of the day, however, was interrupted by the wailing of a siren from a few hundred metres away, out at sea.

"Someone is in trouble," said Liam, a friend who was a part of Freddy's group.

It was not uncommon for an intrepid fun-seeker to venture out too far on a dingy or small motor boat and find the fight with the current too much to handle. Any small boat that becomes disabled off the coastline is left to the mercy of the tumbling waves, while the rescue team makes the journey out to assist. It was never known, at least while Freddy was there, what distress had warranted the intervention of the rescue boat on that particular occasion. The regulars seemed to have taken the occurrence in their stride as for them, a day at Bournemouth was a mixed bag of fun and fright;

though not in equal measure. With the evening slowly drawing to a close, Freddy's chaperone took the group on towards a neighbouring village. The village was to spring a most unusual encounter for the group and for Freddy, in particular.

Later that evening, having absorbed the Bournemouth sunshine and a few servings of seafood dishes, the group were welcoming the more placid nature of the small neighbouring village. Belatedly, it occurred to Freddy that this quaint village had its unique sense of life and like the mythological nymph, it never sleeps. The group were chaperoned into a local café, similarly quaint as the village. Everything was local. Freddy counted seven family-friendly pubs, that were all within a minute or two of each other.

Freddy's ethnicity made him conspicuous by his presence in that café and he was relishing the rarity of it. He was told that Stanley, who shared his ethnicity, would arrive in the café at, or just before, 8:30pm. The visitors could not believe when, true to prediction, Stanley walked in just before 8:30pm and took his place near the serving counter. It would seem as though he came to steal the spotlight from Freddy, as the sole soul brother in the café, on that road, nay, in the entire village. Stanley owned that position, that accolade even. It belonged to him.

Stanley arrived in the village twelve years earlier. Legend has it that he had not left since he arrived. The said legend is yet to establish though, where he came from or where he will go next but in the meantime, he remained a landmark of the village.

Freddy chatted with Stanley for a short while, as he had but a limited time before he should retire for his departure the following sunrise. Everything was quiet as Freddy and the visiting group left the café later that night. Breakfast the next morning was scrambled eggs on toast with tea; English tea please. Freddy left the south coast on the morning train heading back to London with the festivities, the beach, the rescue boat and most memorably, the legend Stanley, irrevocably etched in his mind.

"I shall return," he thought to himself, as the 09:22 train service pulled out of the station at Bournemouth, bound for London Waterloo.

Chapter 14

Fifteen Sheets and Blankets

Before Freddy left Jamaica, he knew that there had always been an amazement about Great Britain and a certain eagerness and desire among many folks from the Caribbean, to visit the UK. This unwavering desire stems from the encounters they had with returning friends and family. Others developed that desire from literature that they read about Great Britain, others from football reports and some became inspired by friends and family who visited on holidays.

There were certain connotations and stereotypes that were ascribed to those who visited or returned permanently. No one could quite understand why the British returnees walked as fast as they did. This was no joke.

"How 'im walk so fast, 'im must be from Inglan'," someone was sure to remark whenever a returnee went walking by.

"An' don't you see that 'im wearing Clarks shoes?" another would add.

These were two of the stand-out features of the British returnees, who had lived in the UK between the time of the *Empire Windrush* and around the late 1980s. There was a strange fascination with the seemingly weird mannerisms, which characterised the actions of the returnees. Coupled with the mannerism was the dress code: a plaid cap, often times some crimplene or corduroy trousers, cotton shirt and a thick jumper. Wearing a thick jumper in thirty-two-degree Caribbean heat must have been their way of remembering the life and fashion of Great Britain. No one could figure it out but such were the tell-tale signs of the returnees during the 1960s, 70s, and up to the 80s. Everyone knew Maas Ronnie, Maas Jacob, Maas Bertie and Maas Felix, in the communities for miles around from where they lived.

As Freddy reminisced on the communal lifestyle that he left in the Caribbean, it made him think of the contrast with his life on the street in London, where he currently lives. He knows not who lives at number 24, while he has lived at number 25 for a few years. And what of number 14, where an occupant comes out at about the same time as he does in the mornings for work? It has been two years now. So far, they have got to "hello," from across the street. Not bad then.

As Maas Felix mingled with old friends and families, he told of his time in the British Army. He, like many others who were recruited during World War 2, had come back home with much to tell to anyone who would listen.

"Inglan' cold you kno," Maas Felix would say.
Freddy was quite young at the time of these tales from the returnees but there is one line from this ex-service man that has stayed with him up to this time. How cold can cold get? There is still no answer for this question, but in one of his communal enlightenments, Freddy remembered hearing Maas Felix panegyrising about the British winter weather.

"I tell you, it cold so bad, that in the night, we had to cover under fifteen sheets and blankets," said Maas Felix.
He did not tell of the combination of sheets and blankets, or if he did, Freddy did not hear. Freddy was just blown away by the sheer number of covering material that Maas Felix had to use to keep warm. The very thought of manoeuvring fifteen sheets and blankets, conjures a picture of some of the ends slipping away from the neck and shoulders. The outermost ones and those underneath must be folding and slipping away from each other. It has to be difficult to grip that combination of material effectively. If Maas Felix successfully manoeuvred fifteen sheets and blankets in one night without the aid of some mechanical lifting apparatus, then he deserves a medal.

Nonetheless, Maas Felix was something of a local treasure. He was the guardian of the community cricket team. In those days, cricket was a way of life for all, especially in rural communities. As Freddy continued to reminisce, he thought of the practice sessions that took place on most weekends, in the playground at the community centre. The pitch would be prepared by the players themselves, as no money was available for specialist groundsmen. However, the pitch preparation never lacked by way of quality. The heavy roller that was pushed and left at one end of the field, was manually rolled out for preparing the batting strip. It is not clear as to the process of getting those rollers to the pitches. The roller was a heavy barrel-sized and cylindrically shaped mass of iron that was a marker at all cricket grounds around the Caribbean. There must have been large shipments of those rollers, from Great Britain, while the game was being exported years earlier around the colonies.

Cricket competitions were frequent from parish to community level. Match day was something of a spectacle. Dozens and in some cases, hundreds, turned out to see these tournaments between neighbouring communities. It was on these days that Maas Felix was in his element. He, leaving home early, would make his way out to the match venue with great pride. His attire, along with his physical presence, were as much about his love of the game, as they were about the advertisement for the game.

For those who for whatever reason may not have heard of the particular game, or if they needed reminding, his stately walk, going past the houses along the road, was an unpaid advertisement.

"Maas Felix, whey dey 'aving match t'day?" was a sure question that would be asked.

Taking this as his chance to perform his duty as community cricket emissary, Maas Felix would provide the details and hopefully, galvanize another spectator for the match. Resplendent was he in his boots designed for the role of umpire: tailored black trousers, felt hat and loose white bush jacket. The pockets on his bush jacket served as receptacles for the balls, bails, scissors, ball counters and other accoutrements. An umpire is usually fully prepared while out on the pitch. Maas Felix was the stabilizing figure of the community team. He was also there at away games. Perhaps, to him could be ascribed the title of '*The face of the community sport*', as he lived for the game.

Then there was Maas Ronnie. Upon returning from the UK, he got quite involved in the local community. He was the church choir baritone singer. While living in Great Britain, Maas Ronnie had been exposed to scouting and the Boys Brigade. As a returning resident, he volunteered to run a Boys Brigade club at the local primary school where Freddy was a student. This was on Friday, after school and Freddy can still remember Mass Ronnie teaching them the BB handshake.

The fascination with the mannerisms of the returnees went much further than the communities, in some instances. Some returning residents went back to the communities to retire peacefully. Others, who had acquired access to educational training through the army, alongside some on their own, returned to take up jobs as teachers, building supervisors, bookkeepers and business owners.

Within whichever field of endeavour they went, the fascination was the same. There were so many unanswered questions, as to why they all had similar characteristics. In addition to the returnees in his community, Freddy had another encounter a few years later with Mr Steele, who was his Economics teacher in sixth form college. 'Steelie', as they nicknamed him, was a returnee, who had gone to the UK in the 1940s. He served with the RAF and after being demobbed, enrolled for a degree in Economics.

It was no wonder when Freddy started sixth form college and had Mr Steele as his Economics teacher, that the news filtered down quickly from the previous batch of students, that Mr Steele is a war veteran. The news also contained an update and forewarning of the 'dos and don'ts' that must be observed in his lessons.

Freddy had walked in on a conversation between Denzil, who was in final year, and Richie and Junior, who were Freddy's classmates, as they were being briefed about what to look forward to in the months ahead.

"Let me see your timetable," Denzil asked.
Junior handed the sheet of A4 paper to him. The paper had the list of classes that Richie, Junior and Freddy would be attending. All three boys were sharing classes in the same three subjects. They had chosen to do Geography, Economics and History. Denzil studied the paper and then proceeded to enlighten them on what was to be expected.

"Alright, I see that you are doing Geography, Miss Smith gets on well with everyone. I had her last year," Denzil told them.

His tone was quite comforting, as Freddy and his two friends read that to be a good sign of things to come.

"I don't know about History," Denzil continued.

"Some of my friends did History last year and they had loads of reading to do, they complained all year."

"Economics is with Mr Steele, get ready for the ride," Denzil said, with an air of the self-appointed, unofficial course advisor.

"He is an ex-soldier; he will tell you about his war experience. Don't ask him too much. He is strange. He is in a world of his own," pontificated Denzil.

If, on other occasions the analysis of the returnees was understandable, in Mr Steele's case, the labels ascribed to him were unjustifiable. What the students did not understand was that there was something known as *post-traumatic stress disorder*.

Looking back now, Freddy could see how insensitive the school community was, or ignorant perhaps. They understood little, if anything, of Steele's emotional state of mind and conferred on him that status of a Jamaican who was in the 'motherland', went to the war and came back as a 'strange' returnee. Freddy could not help feeling some annoyance as he looked back on the stereotyping of the returnees, a stereotype which rendered Mr Steele as 'strange'. The same annoyance was felt for his classmates, who, in their boyish naivety, did more to worsen Steele's state of mind, than anything else.

What Mr Steele divulged was that he migrated for loyalty reasons, as a young man in the 1940s. He joined the military to fight for "Queen and Country" and was soon a part of the RAF.

Apart from his stories, he had some photos to prove that he actually served in the RAF. Freddy had a close relationship with "Steelie" and was privileged to see a smartly adorned Steele, about twenty something years old, standing in crisp formation with his colleagues, in full RAF fatigue. He looked quite impressive and the image stayed in Freddy's mind. The photos were of pale colour as the world of instant colour pictures as it is now, was not the same then. Where colour was used, it was still low-level technology. The photos were pale in comparison to the sharp, clear and glossy camera output that are digitally produced nowadays.

In his distinctively deep staccato voice, "Steelie" did share some of his war time manoeuvres with Richie, Junior and Freddy.

"I was in Korea one time, where I did some fighting, four of us were ambushed and there was a bit of shooting," he once told them. "It was dark, very dark; I could hardly see my colleagues and there were gun shots everywhere, but luckily, we managed to get away," the war veteran reported.

He had a very human side that many did not see. It should come as no surprise that upon hearing of his death, a few years later, that Freddy was deeply saddened as he pitied the ignorance of the boys in his class and the wider school population.

*****

Those formative years presented so much of Great Britain in so many areas of life. The trucks everyone knew in Jamaica were Bedford and Albion Leyland, out of Great Britain. A car passing on the street was likely to be something of the Ford variety: Capri, Consul, Zephyr, Zodiac or a Cortina L, XL or GXL and there was the Morris Austin. British wonder and dominance was ever present, as even in the households, the name 'Electrolux' was on the refrigerator and 'Morphy Richards' was somewhere on an appliance. The Clarks shoes from "Inglan" were properly cleaned and stored in a box, somewhere beneath the bed. Great Britain commanded the attention of everyone and so many Islanders had to see this magical place called "Inglan". Great Britain was attractive to Jamaican nationals, despite how unusual the returnees were thought to be.

Chapter 15

Buffalo Soldier

The military was an attraction for Jamaican nationals in the 1940s. That attraction has never gone away. While the likes of Mr Steele and Maas Felix had joined the British military in the Twentieth Century, Jamaican nations have continued to join the British military in the New Millennium.

Many migrants to the UK are able to speak of a friend or family member, who is now serving in the British military. Whatever the reason, the Caribbean Islands are still providing service men and women for the British military. The army provides skills-training, and this may have lured some job seekers to enlist. Freddy had known Sonia from Jamaica, as a second cousin by his paternal ancestry. Sonia had also moved to the UK in the New Millennium and within a year, she had signed up for the military. She enrolled in the Military nurse-training programme and soon became a qualified nurse.

Having left secondary school a few years earlier, Sonia was determined to move to "Inglan". This was a determination to make her family proud and it was a sentiment that was echoed hundreds of times in the Caribbean, by ambitious juveniles and young adults. Sonia lived in the Midlands of the UK but kept in contact with her cousin, Freddy, by telephone and emails. She had shared the idea of joining the military with Freddy who, as cousins do, discussed the pros and cons of that decision. In the end, he supported her decision. She was fully aware of the fighting which involved the UK troops in Afghanistan and Iraq. However, in a bid to fulfil a personal ambition, she applied to serve and was hitherto recruited into Her Majesty's army.

Freddy heard little from her during her training. He was mostly updated through messages from Sonia's family and in particular, Gregory, her husband. The training programme must have been rigorous, as by way of some correspondence from Gregory, Freddy gleaned that she had not taken to the training in the same manner in which a duck takes to water. However, she finally graduated as a member of the armed forces and was on her way to receiving her military nurse qualification, or some title like that. She had become nurse Sonia and soldier Sonia.

Freddy and soldier-nurse Sonia corresponded more frequently after the training. Family and friends of hers were mindful that there were two on-going wars, where British personnel were heavily involved. In a few months after completing training, cousin Freddy got some news from Sonia that was being anticipated. Despite everyone's anticipation of the news, when it came, they all felt and shared a collective numbness and consternation.

"I got some news today," she told Freddy on the phone.

"I will have to do some months over in Iraq, I am leaving next week," she informed him.

"Really?" said he.

His response was triggered out of fright more than out of misunderstanding.

"Yes, I will be packing soon, you should come and see us before I go."

As she lived with her family on the military base in the Midlands of the UK, Freddy made himself available to go and see her. They were all fully aware of the risk of going to war. The worry was somewhat minimised as she was going primarily as a nurse and frontline fighting, would only be out of absolute necessity.

Sonia's daughter, almost oblivious to the risk of what her mother was about to embark on, or she had become resigned to the reality and nature of her mother's job, stoically went about her business. Whichever it was, no one knew for certain but she dealt with it in her own stride.

Sonia's friends also took consolation, as they were assured that she was going in the capacity of a nurse rather than as a frontline combatant. Freddy made his own contribution to her trip to war, with a gift of a T-shirt. He had recently received a T-shirt with a large portrait of Bob Marley on the front. This shirt was given to him by his brother a few days earlier and Sonia had seen the shirt and liked it. Cousin Freddy felt that he should offer it to her as a token of good fortune, so he did.

"I am going to give you the shirt, here, take it with you," he pleaded.

A T-shirt on its own merit, may not have seemed like a charmed gift, however, the portrait of the late reggae superstar, Bob Marley, brings a direct relevance for a soldier as Sonia. Bob Marley posthumously released a song called 'Buffalo Soldier'. The song pays tribute to the "Buffalo Soldiers" who were a black platoon fighting in the Spanish-American War. Sonia was no Buffalo Soldier but the T-shirt was a deeply symbolic gift for a Jamaican girl, going off to a War Zone.

Freddy received a letter from Sonia, sent back from Iraq, five weeks after she had left for the assignment. Suffice it to say, the letter relayed less than detailed accounts of her mission but that was expected. The details of what happened in Iraq would have been clandestine military information, which could not be divulged to all and sundry.

Sonia had left in July and she was back for Christmas. Freddy found himself on the receiving end of war tales, yet again. He heard the stories from Maas Felix. He heard another account from Mr Steele and now cousin Sonia was about to add her tale from the frontline – the Iraqi frontline.

Hers was a narrow escape on the final morning of her assignment in Iraq. As she and her colleagues waited for the RAF chopper to take them to the airport, they were to have a most unceremonious send off.

"We were so happy to be coming home," Sonia told Freddy, "we were singing and looking at photographs of family from home, just counting down the hours to arrive here," she added.

Her cousin listened intently.

"The RAF Apache wasn't far away, as we could hear the humming of the engine," she continued.

Freddy suspected that this was not going to be a happy tale.

"We had just taken up our duffle bags and personal items when someone shouted, 'in-coming!' " she said. "We barely had time to run before a rocket-propelled grenade landed a few metres away from where we stood," she explained.

Listening to her, Freddy realised that this was a very close encounter, any closer and the outcome may have been different.

"We ran towards a different building but another RPG came at us, and as we ran, we fell in a pool of mud," Sonia concluded mechanically.

With the muddied tunic and soaked boots, she and her colleagues had arrived back home. Sonia remained in the UK and began working at a hospital somewhere in the Midlands.

From Maas Felix and Mr Steele to Sonia, the story is the same. These Jamaicans had joined the British military and served for "Queen and Country". New Millennium technology and frequent trips back home in the Twenty-first Century is creating a better understanding of the British customs and returning residents to the other side of the Atlantic are becoming less "strange" in the eyes of the locals.

Chapter 16

Home away from Home

The Jamaican Diaspora found it necessary to create a connection, to preserve the culture when they migrated. Jamaicans adapted to the new way of life in Great Britain but all the while, keeping alive the ideologies of their own indigenous country.

Take Barnie for instance. Barnie was one of the workers at Rico's barber shop and that made him part of the immediate family at Rico's. As Freddy would spend much of his free time hanging out at the barber shop, he became an extended family member. He was able to assess the acceptance and rejection of *foreign* norms and cultural practices, by the Jamaican Diaspora who frequented the barber shop.

Freddy had gone to the barber shop one Saturday in time to hear a discussion about food choices. There were several takeaway restaurants in close proximity to the barber shop, however, they were not all popular with the Diaspora. Among the regulars, there was a kind of agreement as to which takeaway had met general approval.

"It gone pas' lunch time, I mus' get some lunch now," one customer said, as he waited for a haircut on the lounge chair.

"We goin' order lunch now from Mickey and he will bring it down here," replied Barnie.

"What time him comin'?" the customer asked.

"Not long, he will come in half an hour," Barnie assured him.

Considering that half an hour could mean one hour in Caribbean time, this was little assurance for the customer.

"Half an hour is too long, I am hungry, I will just go an' get a kebab 'cross the road and pick up some salad in the off licence next door," he said.

"What! Kebab? You can't eat kebab man." Barnie said with much emphasis. "That is not our thing man, better if you wait on Mickey food."

"Wha' kind of food Mikey bringin'?" the customer enquired.

"Chicken with boiled dumplins and rice or you can get rice and peas," replied Barnie.

All this time, Freddy remained quiet, as Barnie tried to keep the customer committed to his cultural cuisine. Barnie was not too concerned about the customer's immediate hunger, as long as, as far as Barnie was concerned, he did not go for a different cultural food choice.

Freddy was more of an explorer and had tried

different kinds of food. He had tried the Doner kebab in the past, to see what it was all about. But, standing in the midst of a hungry customer and a Barnie, who had no passion for a dish that was outside his cultural identity, Freddy was between a rock and a hard place. He attempted, however, to mediate and in the end, the hungry customer went across the street to get himself a Doner kebab.

The customer had come back with his meal and had finished eating. The other customers and staff were still waiting for their delivery from Mickey. Freddy was now sitting on the lounge seat in the waiting area, leafing through the local paper, when he heard Rico's landline ringing. It was the delivery man who worked for Mickey.

This was over half an hour since the client was told to wait for half an hour. The message from the phone call was to inform those who had ordered lunch, that the lunch was on the way and would arrive in fifteen minutes. Half an hour had crept up to forty-five minutes in total time. Time among the Diaspora can be elastic. "Soon come" was (and still is) a common response to questions about arrival among the Diaspora and "soon come" can mean anywhere from five minutes to… "won't come".

When Freddy left the barber shop about twenty minutes later, the food had not arrived. He was sure, however, that the food would "soon come".

As Freddy and other Jamaicans who arrived in the New Millennium would find out, the cultural acclaim to indigenous food went beyond the Jamaican Diaspora. Their visits to the regional markets around London, was a testament. Inside the markets, each ethnic group of customers go towards the food stall that sells the food that match their ethnicity. The vendors are usually fully prepared. The African stalls at a market in London will be selling matoke, smoked chicken and ingredients for making garri. Stalls catering for the Mediterranean customers will have apricots, dates, dried vegetables, olives and lamb. The Caribbean stalls will do a selection of ground crops such as sweet potatoes, yams, dasheen and pumpkins.

Freddy and his colleagues soon realised that the stalls were operated mainly by Asian traders. The traders, realising that the ethnic groups are increasing in numbers, started to import from a variety of international exporters. Freddy was shocked at first, when he saw that his yam seller was from Pakistan. On one occasion, he decided to quiz one of the Asian sellers about the source of his stock.

"Where do you get your range of Caribbean food that you selling?" Freddy enquired.

"Brazil, we buy from Brazil, anything we want, import everything," he replied.

"Where you from?" he then asked Freddy, with a hint of pride in the service he was providing for the Diaspora groups.

"Jamaica," Freddy told him.

"We sell food for you," he responded. "I have many customers like you, they come every week, they buy, they like, they come again. Very good customers," he declared.

He seemed quite at ease, as he made his fame and

popularity known to Freddy.

"Any food you want, you don't see, just tell me, I get for you," he said, quite reassuringly.

After a brief chat, Freddy left that stall in the market, still thinking about the emergence of these shops. His mind took him to the days of the early migrants, especially those from the Caribbean Islands. How did they get their favourite ground crops? The journey back and forth took a much longer time and trips back for holidays were infrequent. Invariably, friends and family returning from holiday would take back some indigenous food.

That was in the Twentieth Century. Things had moved on a great deal by the time migrants arrived from the Caribbean Islands in the Twenty-first Century. Freddy was quite impressed by the availability of these indigenous food supplies in the markets and was spellbound by the arrangement of the goods on the stalls. Never before had he seen the particular kind of art employed in the display of the foods. He found himself stopping randomly to admire the layout of fruits, food and meat, on each occasion that he goes into one of these London food markets.

To begin, the fruits are set out with a certain technique, skilfully assorted into bundles, to form a battalion of symmetrical shapes. The cuts of meat have an intriguing arrangement of their own. The steak for roasting has its own cut and is arranged like slats of a venetian blind when closed, in a designated segment of the meat table. The steak for barbeque has its own cut. The pork for grilling has its own cut. Ribs, bellies, loins, shoulder and head, are all exotically laid out for sale.

Home away from home for the Diaspora, who have made the UK and more so London, their home. Everything at their disposal. Twenty-first Century globalisation and the commercial enterprise of traders, help to preserve that piece of ethnic cultural identity. The rainbow of cultures in the UK, brings a range of cuisine from far-flung places of the earth, to converge in one city and sometimes on one street. Diaspora groups have the opportunity to expand their culinary horizons, without travelling to the five main continents.

Twentieth Century migrant Jamaicans especially, have brought their own impact to add to the myriad of spectacles and intoxicating scenes that exist in the city of London. Whatever the Diaspora groups may preserve as their own, the co-existence of cultures brings together, cultural iconography from the Middle East, Asia, Africa, North and South America and Europe, so that a little piece of "home" can be enjoyed in the UK.

Chapter 17

Four Bands

The title 'Intrepid Freddy' could be ascribed to Freddy, for he made good on his endeavour to understand the mystique of "Inglan", whilst at the same time understanding the impact of the Jamaican Diaspora on Great Britain. No one saw better than Freddy how the diversity of cultures that exist in the UK, shape the social landscape of most parts of the country. It must have been late June or early July one year that Freddy attended a concert in North London, at a place called Tottenham. It was the New Millennium and the concept of the concert may not have been conceivable in the previous decades, where each Diaspora group held its own localised entertainment events.

Four bands, four different genres of music, four sets of musicians; all coming together in one venue to showcase their music. Freddy was anxious to see how this musical spectacle would unfold. He would not have missed this for - for a good cup of tea. The music connoisseur that he is, is the motivation for him to widen his knowledge about music from around the world. He has always been fascinated by the range of flavours and varieties of music on the South American continent and still trying to unravel the origins and preservation of beats and tunes that appear in that continent; especially those genres that are still outside of mainstream music. Freddy's personal research on music tells him of the collection of musical instruments that remain local to places in Europe, the middle East, Africa and the Aborigine scrublands of Australia. All of this is, in a word, fascinating.

Without social media, many indigenous world music that fall outside of the mainstream genres would never be heard of and made known to outsiders. This was one of the reasons why the concert that was about to take place was significant for him, as it harnessed a pool of music genres that were indigenous to different cultures, from different parts of the world.

With four bands getting ready to perform, expectation was high. As the hall became packed, Freddy could only think how, by the very nature of the billing, a four-way intermingling of cultures was about to take place. As he reflected on London as told to him by some of the early pioneers, he kept thinking that the social scene had indeed changed. The stories of the early Diaspora included tales of verbal abuse and less than savoury encounters with other local groups. However, standing in this building, on the edge of being immersed into a musicologist's dream, he felt thrilled and proud.

There was a hubbub of voices. The commingled noises were reminiscent of the sound of machines that were running simultaneously in a factory. As the various groups carried on with their different conversations, the first band was being set up.

"Are you ready?!" yelled the MC.

"Yeaah!" replied the ethnically-diverse crowd, who had been waiting in anticipation.

Something special was about to be delivered - a musical package such as none of the patrons had seen before. The first band was introduced and there was the first riff of a revving guitar, as the high tempo rock sounds emanated from the speakers that were laid at both sides of the stage.

The atmosphere in the concert hall was electrifying, as the head-banging beat of the set was pulsated to a crescendo. And what of the singing? Freddy could no more than hear a series of cries, wails and moans from the singer on stage, who was English, obviously steeped in his rock and having the trademark adornments about his person of a true legendary 'rocker'. The band did a few more high-pitched numbers in synchronicity with the hair-flashing, head-rocking, feet-stomping, and air-guitar-playing crowd. Strangely, the Caribbean man was enjoying the arrangement and style of something he had not paid close attention to before, as it was not at the heart of his culture.

There must have been others like Freddy, who found the experience enlightening. The organisers must have hoped for this kind of appreciation amongst the crowd.

Everyone was sure to, even if fortuitously, take notice and possibly develop an awareness and liking for a different genre of music. It was the Twenty-first Century and British nationals were taking notice and participating in *foreign* cultural affairs.

Band number two was connected and ready to put another genre of music on display. With the MC's introduction over, the new band began. The diverse crowd was caught up in pop music – the genre that was most commonly known.

Freddy's high expectations of the event were kept buoyed by the arrival of the Afro-expressions band, from the West African Diaspora. The crowd was swooned by the blending of voices, accents and composition of the Afro-beats. Freddy watched in amazement as the rock and pop die-hard fans, who had remained, were gaining a live and direct exposure to this Afro-centric genre of music.

But save the best for last. Freddy, like most of the music connoisseurs, had stayed to see and hear the last of the four bands. It was mind-boggling for most of the fans in that diverse crowd, to understand how a few old oil containers could be recovered and cut, shaped and battered into formation to create a genre of music. It was a genre produced in someone's back yard, without the use of high-tech equipment.

"Are you ready for the final performance?" the MC shouted.

With the level of appreciation still running high, the diverse crowd replied in the affirmative.

"Please welcome the steel pan sound of Trinidad and

Tobago!"

These instruments, or more precisely, this instrument - for they were all the same - was the most ingenuous creation of sound there was at the event. Freddy could see no difference between the two sets of instruments on the stage. There was one set of old oil containers in one corner and another set of old oil containers in the other corner. Old oil containers cut in half or cut a foot or so away upwards from the bottom around the circumference and then cleaned up, were the only instrument.

The exposed surface of the lid is systematically beaten downwards to form a series of dips and ridges across the entire surface of the lid. The keen ear of the tuner comes into play as each area that is sunk, produces a distinct sound when hit by the sticks. The sticks are capped at one end (the end used for striking), with rubber.

Whatever language or musical persuasion one may belong to, the intuitiveness of this genre is astounding. Freddy knew a bit about music and he could tell that the sounds were in sync and the combination of high and low pitches from those old oil containers, now made into drums, was mesmerising. The drums talked. They spoke a strange language, echoing the strains from a distant memory - a memory of the ancestors. They talked of the hills, of the valleys, the planting of crops, the harvesting thereof, the fires, ropes, chains, whips, of a more serene yet spirited acclamation of - of an identity. An identity of a people. The black people. An uprooted people.

Migrants from the Caribbean and elsewhere, discovered that cultural food and music will always be preserved, so that each Diaspora group can experience the homeland spirit, kept alive by these cultural elements. To keep this experience alive, musicians are sometimes invited from the Caribbean Islands to perform the cultural songs from the homeland, for the Diaspora in the UK.

With four different genres of music playing in the same venue, Freddy and the others in that culturally-diverse group, left the venue with an eclectic musical enlightenment, as four genres of music were put together to celebrate multiculturalism in London in the New Millennium. The mixed crowd had a chance to understand and appreciate one aspect of their neighbour's culture and what identifies each Diaspora as being unique.

Chapter 18

Epsom Derby

Freddy had been exploring the rich variety of the British cuisine, music, customs and identifying features and he found that the country generally, London in particular, is a multicultural centre. People from different cultural heritage have extended their search for a new experience in Great Britain. Some have embraced quintessential British pastimes, such as flower fairs, air shows, antique auctions, tea parties, cricket club membership and football season ticket subscription.

But what the New Millennium migrants discovered, is that some of these British cultural events are still predominantly attended by native English patrons. The world-famous Chelsea flower show, which is held in London, is a colourful and intriguing display of flowers in bloom. The show usually runs for five days during the Spring time and it is common for over one hundred and fifty thousand visitors to attend the display during that time. On the occasion that Freddy made his visit to the event, his ethnicity was made conspicuous by the low numbers of the Caribbean Diaspora at the show.

Attendance to other British cultural events, such as air shows, is also limited. Air shows usually take place in counties away from London, where ethnic groups are in much smaller numbers than they are in London. Shoreham, which is famous for these shows, is approximately sixty miles away from London and the town itself had nearly fifty thousand residents in 2015. From Freddy's research, he realised that the combined percentage of minority ethnic Diaspora, in Shoreham in 2015, was less than five percent.

The arriving Caribbean Islanders may not have been drawn towards some of these British cultural events, for reasons such as geographical distance, or a limited desire to engage in an altogether *foreign* cultural pastime. Some Jamaicans, especially the New Millennium migrants, may have memories of "Kite-flying" - a national pastime in the Caribbean Islands that has become a cultural extravaganza. The air shows in Great Britain would bring a reminder to Freddy and other Islanders as the "Kite-Flying" cultural event is a demonstration of skill, precision, tactics and design technology. The air show is also a show of skill, precision, aircraft design and aviation technology.

The annual "kite-flying" season has been around for decades in Jamaica and was probably introduced to the Island by Chinese immigrants from the Nineteenth Century. The Easter sky is usually crafted into a mosaic spectacle of shapes, colours and sizes, reminding everyone that "kite season" is in full swing; in full flight. The pastime has grown from a community event into a national festival and dozens of kite flyers attend the annual festival to show off some exquisite designs, patterns and ways of flying kites.

In attendance at one of the Easter extravaganza, during his adolescent years, Freddy had merely expected to look at a few kites and go back home. In no way, did he expect that the event would sustain his short attention span for a good five hours, however, the scenes were enthralling. Kite flyers from Germany and Canada and other countries, now look forward to this festival to compete for prizes and the show now has an international appeal.

Although the British air shows have not attracted an overwhelming number of the Caribbean Diaspora, for whatever reason, the Diaspora would be fully appreciative of the skill and artistic patterns formed by man and machine at these air shows. This would be much in the same way that they appreciate the skill and artistic patterns formed by the dozens of kites that are flown at the Jamaica kite festivals, as both events are a piece of cultural heritage.

However, there are some British pastimes that attract hundreds of participants from minority ethnic groups. The 'Sport of Kings' is one celebrated British event that has attracted hundreds of English and various Diaspora groups each year. Freddy and his friends have travelled to see the 'Sport of Kings', to understand how the various cultures in the UK are pulled together by such an event.

*****

Nestled away in the south of the UK is a market town called Epsom, in the county of Surrey, England, 13.6 miles south south-west of London. The annual horse racing derby takes place in Epsom and the sporting event is part of the calendar for different ethnic communities.

Freddy had volunteered for three hours on Saturdays to teach a group of minority ethnic children, in a small centre in the North London borough of Haringey. There were three other volunteer teachers; Steven, Brenda and Shadei. They too were of the Caribbean Diaspora. Steven and Shadei were the second generation of the Twentieth Century Jamaican migrants. Brenda had moved to the UK as a child – thirty-five years earlier. Freddy learned of the derby one Saturday, through a conversation between two of these volunteer colleagues.

"I need to put my list together for Epsom," Brenda said to Steven, as Freddy walked into the classroom where they were.

"I can't miss it," Steven responded, "last year we had a good time."

"I have twenty tickets for sale," Brenda added.
Freddy tried to work out what the discussion was about.

"Put me down for three tickets," Steven told Brenda.

"Freddy, would you like to come to Epsom Derby?"

111

Brenda asked.

"What's that?" Freddy replied.

"It's a big race day that we go to all the time," she said.

"That sounds good but I am not a betting man," responded Freddy.

"No, no," interrupted Steven, "we don't go there to bet," he assured Freddy. "It's a good fun day out where loads of coaches with people from all over the UK come for the day," he explained.

"Alright, yes, sounds like something I would like to see," replied Freddy after a bit of thought.

"You can get a ticket for the coach, as I have twenty left to be sold," Brenda informed him. "Come, you will enjoy it," she concluded.

The conversation continued as the two 'regulars' painted a picture of how the day's excursion was likely to unfold. They would all meet at a certain point in Stamford Hill, from there the coach would move through North-West London and then down towards the South. In fact, there were supposed to be two coaches.

Freddy knew of other derby days, such as the Grand National and Ascot racing. The Epsom derby was just as popular and although it takes place outside of London, it is well attended by several Diaspora groups.

With the expectation of the day's occurrence on his mind, Freddy arrived at Stamford Hill and left his personal transport along a side road and walked around to the parked coaches. This was three weeks after he first heard about this shindig. Steven was already there. The men, who were obviously used to this sort of thing and would have been instrumental in putting the trip together, were packing boxes and other containers into the holding area of the coaches. There were boxes with drinks, a large oven-like container, popularly known as a jerk drum, water bottles, igloos with ice and an assortment of large aluminium food containers, with meat that was prepared overnight and set to marinate.

These he knew were important items for the day ahead, especially as the travelling group were informed that there was no need to take food or drink, as both would be provided.

"All set for the journey?" Steven asked Freddy.

"Yes," he replied, feeling a bit excited upon seeing that the organisers had spared no effort in their preparation.

A few minutes later and they were all boarded. Both coaches headed westwards towards Golders Green and on to the motorway. As they journeyed, Freddy could detect the flavours from the food containers. The salt-fish fritters were handed out to each member of the group on his coach. The same operation was happening on coach number two. Tea and coffee accompanied the first round of food handouts.

Everyone seemed to be in good spirit, from the front to the rear of the coach. Chatter was incessant, punctuated by laughter.

"Las' year this time we were fur'da along," moaned Morgan.

Morgan introduced himself to Freddy later on. He was as a regular on these trips.

"We had less traffic on the road las' time, still it not

too bad, we movin' along," declared Marie; Morgan's wife, "at least we not stuck."

"So longs as the delay doan spoil me derby day," Morgan retorted, "I will be aw'right."

An hour and a half later and they arrived at the race venue. Derby day was definitely on. The coaches were directed towards a wide expanse of open hillside. They parked in the coach enclosure, alongside dozens of other coaches. This section of the race course is known as 'The Hill'. In close proximity were the limousines, cars, minibuses and a few helicopters that had taken other enthusiasts to the derby.

Freddy and his colleagues were now at Epsom Derby but the races were a world away. The races were taking place at another end of the race course. From the distance, they could make out the Queen's Stand and sections of the race track itself but spread across 'The Hill' were numerous fun-seekers, representing a range of ethnic groups. Thinking back to the description given to him by Steven, the reality for Freddy was absolutely accurate. 'The Hill' was a giant picnic. Families in cars and groups who came in coaches, were now preparing their food. Footballs had come out. Cricket bat and ball were out. Tents were going up. Music systems were being strung up. Deck chairs had come out; picnic mats and board games were out too.

The crowd composition ranged from the very old, to the very young; barely able to look outwards into the glare of the sunlight. Then there were the less mobile, whose family helped them onto their Motability scooters, enabling them to wheel themselves through the crowd on 'The Hill'. The excitement was buzzing. Brenda, who had travelled on coach number two, came around to make an announcement. For the crowd on 'The Hill', the other announcements across the race track, were of little or no significance.

"The drinks are now packed onto the ice, so you are free to get what you want from the tent," Brenda announced.

A tent was set up linking the two coaches together. The tent was the refreshment centre for the day. Steven and Freddy went towards the tent for refreshment. With no protection from the sun, they were grateful for the refreshment but it was of little help, as they remained fully exposed to the sun.

In contrast, the occupants of the VIP box over at the race track, had a protected vantage position, shielded from the dazzling summer sunlight, whilst engrossed in the races in front of them, as many would have been owners or breeders of the horses.

Back on 'The Hill', Brenda came around with another announcement. Above the noise, they could just about make out the announcement. The oven-shaped grilling apparatus was by then put to stand between the coaches under the tent. The marinated meat in those aluminium containers, was sizzling away on the grill. The tantalising flavours permeated across the hillside - stimulating the appetite of anyone within a thirty-metre radius. Brenda's call had to be about the food.

"Just so you know, the grilled chicken will be ready soon," Brenda shouted.

Her voice was barely audible above the din.

Other groups along 'The Hill' were doing something similar. Sandwiches and picnic-styled meals were all around. A child with an ice lolly was never far away, as they went about their business in the scorching sun. A game of fun football was in progress. The game had a set of players who just joined in and played football, without knowing the names of their 'teammates'. There was no winning team; it was like a carousel of all different ethnic groups just joining in, playing and leaving at will.

The women in the game made up their own rules, as they pushed the men aside to get possession of the ball. On another day, that would have been a sending off but in the excitement and euphoria that engulfed the throng on 'The Hill', rules were forgotten. The diverse crowd on 'The Hill' could tell very little about the races on that day. They had a day out at Epsom derby, but saw nothing of the derby.

An exhausted but delighted crowd eventually left the 'The Hill' late on that Saturday afternoon. Horses ran, races were won and dividends paid out. That was a world away from the picnic on 'The Hill' but this was a British cultural event, where the ethnically diverse worlds would collide. Derby day at Epsom brings the various Diaspora groups close together, in a common cultural and social setting.

Chapter 19

The Hidden Fascination

"The name's Bond, James Bond." Now where did Freddy hear these words? They were from the '007' archives of the James Bond series. The famous line symbolizes the suave and poise of agent '007'; James Bond, the fictional British spy. Equally important, is the fact that these words have a lasting connection with the Caribbean Island of Jamaica.

How did that happen? An appetite for the Island amongst the British, developed in the 1940s and as the *Empire Windrush* generation were making their way from the Island of Jamaica, some English ex-service men, were making their way to the Island of Jamaica.

The writer of the James Bond novels, Ian Fleming, having been to Jamaica on military business during World War 2, decided that after the war, the Island would be his second home. The secret of his fascination with the Island must be underlined by the intrigue and natural beauty of the Island's alluring sandy beaches and deep green forest vegetation. In addition to the natural beauty, is the weather; seasonal rainfall and average annual temperature of 30 degrees Celsius. Those natural beguiling elements have made the Island consistently popular with British investors, tourists and retirees, looking for a tropical retirement.

Ian Fleming kept his word and bought property in Jamaica, in the parish of St. Mary, when the war was over. His passion for writing grew, as he occupied a piece of the natural landscape known as 'Goldeneye', which inspired Fleming to write his first book. His first book was written at his new home in Jamaica. The novel, *'Casino Royale'* was a success. Fleming wrote his second Bond novel in Jamaica, *'Live and Let Die'*. His third novel, *'Moonraker',* was also written in Jamaica.

Jamaica was undeniably proving to be a source of inspiration for Mr Fleming, as his fourth novel, *'Diamonds are forever',* was written in Jamaica too. Indeed, his fifth novel entitled, *'From Russia with Love'*, was, predictably, written in Jamaica. Ian Fleming went on to write a total of twelve novels in Jamaica and the connection between the famous Bond line and Jamaica, came about as these novels were adapted into film. This is one gift of Jamaica to the British arts culture. The reciprocal interest and attraction between the two countries live on in the New Millennium and this reality answers the question that Freddy and the Jamaican Diaspora have been asked on countless occasions.

"How could you leave such a nice hot country in the West Indies and come to England?"

*****

Freddy found himself at a post office on a very cold January day in London. Despite being inside the building, the thickly padded coat and headgear were little match for the blistering cold. Almost everyone who walked in from the high road, had numb fingers. A customer of English ethnicity standing behind him in the queue thought that she had to share her view of the day's weather with someone. She chose Freddy.

"Cold init?" she asked. "This is one of them very cold winters," she stated.

Before Freddy could reply, the woman continued her lamentation.

"Last time I was cold like this was up in Huddersfield with my daughter," she continued, "really cold up there."

With the cold rooted deep in his body, Freddy could only manage to nod in acknowledgement of what she had to say. This must have encouraged the woman, as the commentary shifted from the weather to her family.

"When my daughter comes down here, she says 'mum, it's not cold down here, why are you complaining so much?' Her children are just the same, they always say I should come to Huddersfield more often, so I can get used to the cold," she said.

Freddy returned the same response, by nodding his head in a show of acknowledgement.

"Have you lived in England long, I see that's a good warm jacket you're wearing," the woman intimated.

Before he, or she, could continue the conversation, the voice came from behind the post office counter, "Next in line please!"

Freddy needed to get to the counter and get out quickly but he managed to give her a brief reply.

"Yes, it's warm, thanks. I have lived here for a long time, so I dress warm to face the cold," he told her with a situational smile.

"So, where are you from?" she asked, oblivious to the call from behind the counter, which meant it was Freddy's turn to be served.

She had an opportunity to talk and she was making good use of that.

Freddy moved to the counter but he continued the conversation while they were both being served next to each other; she at counter number four and he, at counter number three. The ultimate question did come while they were at the counter and as with the case of the *Empire Windrush* generation, he was asked about leaving a warm country with 'good' climate to be in the cold weather of the UK.

"Jamaica," replied Freddy.

"Now why would you leave such a nice warm country to come to England?" she enquired. "I have never been there but I hear it's very nice and you have sunshine all year round," she declared. "Why you leave?" the woman questioned.

Freddy gave her some kind of answer to appease her, before they both left the post office; he, going one direction and she, going another.

The frequent repetition of that comment about the beautiful weather of the Caribbean, shows the kind of appreciation there is for the Islands. It is that Island appeal that attracted Ian Fleming to the Caribbean.

*****

As Ian Fleming went about his writing, English playwright and composer, Sir Noel Coward, also made Jamaica his second home. It may have been the weather, the lush vegetation or the natural beauty of the landscape that caused the British composer and actor, Ivor Novello, to make Jamaica his new home. This was long after Australian-born actor, Errol Flynn, had made Jamaica his second home, by settling in a district close to where Fleming and Novello would eventually live. English businessman, Chris Blackwell, bought property in Jamaica, from where he invested in the local reggae music industry.

The reciprocal interest plays out in the streets of the UK on a daily basis. The indigenous reggae music can be heard at high volume in cars driven by ethnic Asian migrants and Europeans alike. The love for the Jamaican music, which is a cultural feature, goes back to the late 1960s and the 1970s, when bands playing this ethnic minority genre of music, were invited to entertain the British fans. One of the best known invited reggae bands in the Twentieth Century, is 'The Wailers', who had their stand out performance at the Lyceum theatre in 1975, to a largely English audience.

The British and European attraction for Jamaican culture in the Twenty-first Century, goes far beyond the music. Some English and European neighbours of Jamaicans in the UK, have been invited to Jamaican barbeques and have developed a penchant for the signature jerk chicken, patty and rice and peas. To go along with the English and European appreciation for the music and food, is the fascination with the Jamaican dialect, often used by the Diaspora. There have been many anecdotes about the broken English of the Jamaican Diaspora and the way it is spoken and interpreted.

The broken English spoken by the Caribbean Diaspora groups in general, is sometimes difficult to understand and translate. A native English speaker, having a conversation with a Caribbean national in the native dialect, will be left a few yards behind in trying to decipher the broken English. Even among the Islanders, the broken expressions and speech patterns vary so much that Diaspora groups from each Island, find it challenging to understand one another.

Freddy had made friends with other Caribbean nationals in the UK, in his first few years. Kesman was one such friend, whom he met through a family contact. Kesman is a Trinidadian national. They had not seen each other for some years and Freddy must have forgotten about his variety of broken English and his speech pattern, as when they ran into each other four years later, Freddy had to go through the ritual of nodding and smiling, so as to appear to be keeping up with some of Kesman's expressions. The Trinidadian version of broken English is a speedy variety that has an undulating intonation which makes it – melodious; it's like music to the ear. Each Caribbean Island has its own unique cultural pattern and version of broken English.

Despite the difference between the Standard English and the Caribbean cultural versions of broken English, there is an underlying appreciation for the Caribbean dialects by the English nationals. The appreciation extends beyond interactions in the communities and shared places of work, to the education system. School teachers arriving from Jamaica to the UK in the New Millennium, discovered that the Caribbean dialect was part of the English curriculum. The arriving teachers were shocked as much as they were proud, to see cultural dialect being used for British educational studies.

The discovery of the dialect in school literature, was most profound for those teachers who taught English, as there were poems in the General Certificate School Examination (GCSE) anthology, of extreme Jamaican dialect, written by Benjamin Zephaniah. And there were prose writings too, with the Jamaican cultural dialect, that were stacked in the libraries and listed on students' recommended reading list.

Benjamin Zephaniah has made a name for himself as a poet and novelist, who writes in Jamaican dialect. Benjamin Zephaniah was one of the chosen poets whose work was studied by students of all ethnicities in Great

Britain, as they studied for national British exams. The GCSE anthology had the work of other poets, such as John Agard, who writes in a Guyanese dialect and Grace Nichols, who is also a native Guyanese.

The British interest in Jamaican cultural elements developed in the Twentieth Century, from Fleming's fascination with 'Goldeneye', to the fixation with the music, food and dialect in the Twenty-first Century. The Jamaican teachers could see the impact of the dialect on the British education system; an impact that stems from the dominance of the Jamaican culture in Great Britain, in the New Millennium.

Chapter 20

New Investments

It was London that had the largest Caribbean Diaspora from the time they arrived on the *Empire Windrush*. As the years went by, some members of the group decided that they would set up businesses to serve the needs of the Diaspora. However, by the time Freddy arrived in the United Kingdom, the number of Caribbean businesses paled in comparison with the Turkish, Polish, Greek or Asian-run shops along the streets.

Freddy had a bit of difficulty identifying the different European shop keepers, in his first few months in the UK. He would say one race and Reggie from Rico's barbershop would always help him to clarify the identity of the various European ethnic groups, with whom Freddy came into contact.

"No man, he is Turkish," Reggie would say, "everyone working in that shop is Turkish," Reggie frequently pointed out.

On other occasions, Freddy would be schooled on the identity of other ethnic groups.

"You see all those shops on that road, they are Greek people shops," Reggie would explain, with an air of anthropological superiority.

"Over dat side you ave the Indian shops and di Pakistani shops, doan mix them up cause dey doan like dat," Reggie would also say.

The new migrant in town, soon learned the differences between the range of nationalities that he encountered from day to day, especially in the commercial sector. From his boyhood days, Freddy could remember that shopkeepers in the Jamaican communities were mainly indigenous Caribbean natives or Chinese.

The local shop, which served everyone for miles around as he was growing up, was owned by a Chinese family. It was also common to find the petrol stations, wholesalers, haberdasheries, supermarkets and bakeries, to be owned and operated by a Chinese family. Anecdotal it may be, perhaps, that the owner was usually referred to as 'Mr Chin', a title that they accepted and responded to, regardless of their actual surname. But this was the custom.

'Mr Chin' found favour with all and sundry and he was the hub of the domestic grocery life. He also acted in many instances as judge and jury for petty disputes among some regular customers. The successful run of business by the Chinese, had its beginnings from the arrival of immigrant labourers who travelled to Jamaica and other Caribbean Islands in the 1840s. Chinese businesses became an iconic feature of Jamaica's commercial landscape in the Twentieth Century and is still quite noticeable today.

Fast forward to Great Britain, twenty odd years later and Freddy arrives to a significantly different demographic landscape; the shopkeepers' names have changed and 'Mr Chin' was hardly seen. All Jamaican migrants to the UK had to adjust from 'Mr Chin's shop', to shops whose operators were more European in nature. New migrants had to get used to the difference; and fast. Freddy was grateful to Reggie for his race identification lessons, as he realised the embarrassment it may have caused to refer to any of the new breed of merchants wrongly.

Friends of the Jamaican Diaspora soon developed a taste for the imported items and demand for goods from the Caribbean was gaining in popularity. There were now second-generation British-born Londoners and new migrants who invested in restaurants.

The interior of these restaurants had an aura of their own. Standing in a Caribbean restaurant makes for an entertaining fifteen minutes, whilst waiting for a take-away order, or an interesting hour, whilst having a dine-in meal, as there is always a vibrancy among the customers. Quite commonly, the New Millennium migrants found confusion with the ordering of a Caribbean staple of rice with curry and chicken.

"Can I have a chicken curry?" someone would often say.

'Chicken curry' is an Indian dish. 'Curry chicken' is the authentic Jamaican dish which is prepared, consumed and loved by so many and has a distinctively different flavour from the Asian meal of 'chicken curry'.

For the take-away restaurants, where the popular jerk meats are sold, it is common to see plumes of dark, charcoal-laced smoke billowing from the cooking area. This was usually at the back of the building, and the smoke could be seen going upwards against the roof and then mushrooming across the ceiling and with nowhere to go, descends to form an envelope around the waiting customers. All this forms part and parcel of the ambience, preparation and exceptional taste of this Caribbean speciality - Jerk. He who manages to bear with the envelope of smoke, ultimately experiences the taste of the golden-brown, flavourful meat, that is brim-full of secret spices and herbs. The ingredients have been used and enjoyed for many generations of the Diaspora.

By 2010, some Jamaican restaurants started to establish chain stores, particularly in London, as there was more and more demand for the dishes from these ethnically-oriented restaurants.

The new Jamaican migrants in the Twenty-first Century had arrived as the catering service industry was developing to serve the Diaspora. At a wedding reception that Freddy attended, the guests were mainly of a Caribbean heritage and therefore the food of choice was ethnic. The food, he was told, was prepared and delivered by a company that was formed by a Jamaican entrepreneur.

With the Diaspora number rising to hundreds of thousands, catering services have sprung up across

Great Britain, to provide for a range of occasions, including weddings, graduations, funerals, christenings and birthday parties.

Restaurateurs and caterers receive the support of the Caribbean Diaspora, who need to have a reminder of the Caribbean heritage whilst living in a foreign country. Other Diaspora groups who have made Great Britain their home, do their best to find food of their minority ethnic group. Their restaurateurs and caterers provide food for their big occasions such as Eid, Diwali and other cultural celebrations.

Chapter 21

Remittances

The brave Islanders have made the journey to the UK with different hopes and dreams in mind. Some with hopes of fortune, others with dreams of fame or some kind of social change. But, as they left, friends and family who remained behind, had their hopes and dreams too. The financial sacrifices made by families, to help with migration costs, have been eulogised over and over. However, less public eulogising has been offered over the emotional and social sacrifices that were made by the migrants themselves and the families left behind in the Caribbean Islands. There was the cost of paying the passage on the ship (in the case of the *Empire Windrush* generation) and air fare for the later migrants. For any migrant getting on a ship or boarding a plane, there is a sinking feeling - an emotional emptiness at the thought of leaving ailing grandparents and in some cases parents and spouses. However, the greatest pain must come from leaving children behind.

Many children, left behind by those parents who could not travel initially with them, were heart-broken and cried for many days after their parents were gone. Up and down the Islands, the migrating parents made a similar promise to the grandparents who would mind the children.

"As soon as I settle down, I will send for the children," many migrants had famously said.

This was some assurance for the grandparents.

For the loans taken to fund the trips abroad, some were paid back with interest, over the following years. Other family members were saddled with the debt for many years, as little or no money came to service the loans. The reason was that things did not always go according to plan for all migrants. It took much longer for some migrants to pay back loans and take their children to join them.

Freddy grew up and went to school with a few friends whose parents had migrated. As young as they were, they had a certain kind of sympathy for the friends whose parents had migrated but at the same time, there was a strange admiration for them. They sympathised with them, as their parent or parents could not be there to share in their day-to-day ups and down. They were children but they knew that, that was not the desired scenario and the others admired their friends whose parents were away, as they were the ones in the school who would turn up at the start of the term with sleek shoes, trend-setting bags and loads of money to buy lunch for everyone.

Freddy and some friends had a conversation one lunch time, as they waited on the side-lines of the playground for their turn to go out and bat. They were playing cricket, as they did at break and lunch times. Cricket was their sport. Freddy and his friends grew up in the glory days of West Indies cricket, so it is no surprise that that was the game they all lived for as boys. They had their Gary Sobers, their Alvin Kallicharan, their Derryck Murray, their Lawrence Rowe, and their very own Michael 'Hurricane' Holding.

There was so much love for those legendary cricketers, who were role models and that kept the boys trying to emulate the high standards in the Nineteen seventies, eighties and early Nineteen nineties. However, those fortunes of the cricket changed later on.

*****

So, sitting on the side-lines, Freddy and his team mates waited to bat. They batted in order of skill. Freddy batted somewhere... somewhere down the order - way down the order. Sometimes the wait could be long, if the higher order batsmen were in good nick on the day. The waiting batsmen willed the bell to stay silent during their playtime. The bell was only welcome just before break, so that they could get out to play, just before lunch so that they could get out and play again and at the end of school; well...that was time to go home. The bell was an unwelcome enemy to fun, whenever they waited to bat during the lunch hour. On one particular Thursday, it was no different but as they waited to go into bat, Freddy and his friends listened to a conversation between Bob and Michael. Bob's mother had migrated to the UK and rumour had it that Michael's parents were planning to migrate the following year. Both boys were chatting for a while, until the conversation turned to Bob's possessions.

"How many shoes you have?" Michael asked Bob. Everyone knew he must have had quite a few pairs of shoes, for he would often times mention the range of items that came in the barrels from his mother who lived in England.

"Let me see," replied Bob, "mi av a brown one wit lace, a brown one wit buckle, a black one wit high top, one nother black one wit metal on the toe, one blue sneakers, one like cowboy boots..."

The bell rang. What a relief!

In a strange way, the rest of the boys were relieved when the bell rang, as they were exhausted from listening to the list of footwear that Bob owned. Under normal circumstances, they would have rued the sound of the bell as they did not get to bat but now, they felt they could give batting a miss, if it meant they did not have to endure anymore of Bob's litany of shoes ownership.

It was just a strange way of relating to those among them whose parents were away. Bob was popular amongst his peers but it was hard to understand how he could own so many pairs of shoes, when they had one pair. It seemed like, for what Bob was missing, he was compensated by regular packages from the UK. The joy of grandparents and the children, was overwhelming on days when the message came to inform them that barrels had arrived.

Bob spared no opportunity to keep his friends up to date on the items that were expected, or had actually arrived from the UK in barrels.

"Mi not comin school tomorro," he would say.

Then someone would enquiry about his reason for random absence. There was no 'out-of-school' form to be signed. There was no such distinction as 'authorised' and 'unauthorised' absences recorded, as is the case in many schools nowadays. If Bob had to be away, he just had to be away; no documentation required. Phones were not heard of then. So, no expectation either for a phone call into school, regarding absences.

"Why you not comin school tomorro?" someone would ask.

"Mama sen barrel from Inglan," Bob would reply, "an mi goin with gran'ma and papa to Montego Bay at the wharf, to get it," he would explain gleefully.

Only if the conversation was aborted by the bell, or if a teacher was coming, would his friends be spared the details of what was coming from England in the barrel.

The remittance of regular foreign exchange from the UK formed the economic mainstay of the families who remained in the Caribbean. The money would be deposited to savings accounts, used to pay off loans, used for home improvement and used to take care of day to day living expenses.

Occasionally, these remittances do not go towards

the intended use - bank accounts sometimes remained empty - and many woeful explanations sufficed, when those abroad request a financial update.

The continued movement of people in the New Millennium from the Caribbean meant that there was a greater need for two main services - money remittances and shipping services. These two services have become popular all year round, with an increase in demand at Christmas time. The pattern has not changed from how it was when Freddy was in school with Bob.

In the New Millennium, Freddy the boy from school with Bob, has become an adult and resides in the UK - getting a sense of what Bob's mother was experiencing. Freddy's experience has not changed in this century, as it is a common sight to see shipping company trucks along the high roads in the UK and on side roads, looking for addresses, especially at Christmas. Invariably, they are going to collect a barrel or a crate to ship back to friends and family from the Diaspora in Britain. What might be different, however, is that children might not be pulled out of school randomly, as before, to make the trip to the wharf.

The shipping of barrels is one feature of the Diaspora and their relationship with the Caribbean Islands. Money remittance is another feature of the Diaspora and their relationship with family and friends in the Caribbean. It seems to be a rapidly spreading business in the New Millennium and a money remittance office is always close to every Caribbean national in the UK. Jamaican Migrants can get news and information that matter specifically to the current Diaspora on community radio stations, so they know which shipping company or remittance service is giving the best deals. Caribbean migrants rarely get information about local bargains from mainstream radio, so minority ethnic radio stations serve the Diaspora well.

Minority ethnic radio stations also provide information for the Diaspora about the opening of new restaurants, or of new menu choices at existing restaurants. The New Millennium migrants, as well as migrants who left Jamaica and other Caribbean Islands in the Twentieth Century, frequently use the remittance and shipment services in the UK. Many more 'Bobs' in the Caribbean Islands, await the arrival of money and another barrel.

Chapter 22

The Road Trips

'Great Britain' means different things to different people and as such, many nationalities migrate to Great Britain. Some of the British attractions like Big Ben, London Eye, Tower Bridge and Buckingham Palace, draw people from different countries to Britain.

For Freddy, it was a combination of factors – a subtle indoctrination from childhood nursery rhymes and adolescent studies of Great Britain, which created a subconscious force for his decision years later, as an adult. When he arrived, there was so much to see and do, that he decided to embark on a road trip around the country. Freddy, up to this point, had been more than an arm-chair traveller and from his real journeys, he had seen the green rolling hills of the countryside and the skyscrapers of the square mile in the capital. He wanted to see more.

*****

Sheffield was the first stop.

The first destination on his series of planned road trips was Sheffield, which was the first large city he visited away from London. Setting out from London on a coach, which was actually his first coach ride, Freddy was quite expectant of things to be seen on the journey. Having done the research, he knew that the coach ride would last between four and five hours and that sounded like an adventure to him. Pulling out of Victoria Coach Station took some time, as the roads were busy with lunch-time traffic. He hoped it was no indication of things to come.

Freddy and the other passengers on the coach eventually left the London congestion behind and were cruising along the motorway, heading for the 'North'.

Relaxed.

The route was scenic.

This was the England that he imagined. The Beatles, Mungo Jerry, Phil Collins; these were some of the names he associated with the feel-good factor of Great Britain. Many a morning, he would tune in to the radio at 8:30am, to hear the million-selling singles on the international music chart. Merely a boy of eleven, maybe twelve, Freddy had an interest in music and what songs were hitting the charts locally and internationally. There was a certain soothing, airy sound and candescent feel in the British songs then, that shaped part of Freddy's expectation of Great Britain.

With his head set back against his seat on the coach, Freddy drifted off into nostalgia and his thoughts roamed.

As he looked out across the open fields, Freddy could see the sheep in the meadow and the cows in the corn and a few stacks of hay.

"I am actually in England," he thought, before pulling himself back to the moment.

A few thoughts later and the coach was pulling into the first rest stop. The passengers had a quick walk around and some refreshment. There was a change of driver and off they went again.

Sheffield beckoned.

Soon it would greet them.

An hour or two later and Sheffield welcomed them.

First, were the seven hills. No one counted them but the introduction to the city included information about the seven hills. The city is said to be built on seven hills. That geographical fact was strange to Freddy, as London is generally flat and that is the city he knew best. The few hills in London are never mentioned as a selling point of that city, as the height of those hills are negligible, when compared to Sheffield. The landscape was the only feature that startled Freddy a little. He was just amazed by those hills, however, within a few hours, he got used to them. He knew not on which of the hills he stayed, as they all looked the same.

Arriving in Sheffield meant that there was a chance for Freddy to see the circus. *'The Circus was in town'*.

Literally. The Russian circus was set to perform in Sheffield, later that day. He had heard of the skill and death-defying stunts that they perform.

Now the time came for the circus performance to begin that afternoon. Walking through the gates felt like going into an ordinary concert but arriving inside that colossal tent was awesome. Seeing circus performances on television was spectacular, however, a live viewing is extraordinary. The thrill-seeking Freddy was astonished by being so close to the action and seeing the flying trapeze performances in front of his very eyes.

"How do they keep to such precise timings?" he wondered.

His breathing came to a standstill each time an acrobat released his grip from another and flies through the air. By some magical spell, the acrobat manages to catch the tips of another acrobat's fingers - or so it appeared - but they never missed a connection. Freddy could only start breathing again when the acrobat grabbed hold of another performer's fingers.

They kept on playing havoc with Freddy's inhaling and exhaling, as the stunts went on for what seemed like all day. He was under immense pressure throughout that performance, as his breathing was involuntarily synchronising with their stunts. This was almost an ordeal but he had volunteered for it – in some way.

The performances with the animals were equally impressive. That though, he knew would cause some debate as there are a range of views about the use of animals in performances. These Russian acrobats were highly skilled and both males and females unnerved, yet entertained the locals of Sheffield and visiting friends.

Sheffield has two well-known football arenas. A trip to Sheffield would not be complete without seeing the iconic football venues, Sheffield Wednesday and Sheffield United. Ensconced between the hills, is the very large landmark stadium of Sheffield Wednesday.

Sheffield Wednesday was a name that sports fans heard repeatedly on the radio in the Caribbean, back in the Twentieth Century. There was the Saturday night sports round-up on the BBC radio channel. Fans of English Football in the Caribbean received weekly updates on the English FA Cup and Division two match scores of the day. Sheffield Wednesday was a regular feature then. There were reports that ran scores sounding like: "Sheffield Wednesday: 2, Everton: 1, or Sheffield Wednesday: 1, Everton: 2". "Nottingham Forest: 0, New Castle United: 4, or Nottingham Forest: 4, New Castle United: 0". These are not precise results but that was the kind of bulletin that came over the radio. Laying before Freddy now, was Sheffield Wednesday Stadium.

*****

Birmingham was next.

Freddy was on a journey to see as much of the rest of the UK as possible and his next road trip was to Birmingham. Birmingham has been an attraction for the Caribbean Diaspora from the Twentieth Century. It lured the early Diaspora, as jobs were available around the coalfields. Outside of London, Birmingham or 'Brum' as the city is more commonly called, has been home to a large Caribbean population and so it was important for Freddy to visit this city, a few months later, in his quest to *discover* Great Britain.

A freezing December weather greeted him. What a contrast to London, as when he left, there was no such substance as snow - just a cold, crisp weather. But, upon arriving in 'Brum' there was a thick covering of snow on the ground and he had left his wellies behind.

There is a joyful atmosphere in the UK, whenever the snow puts in its appearance. To add to this joyfulness, the snow had arrived in 'Brum' for Christmas, making it a 'white Christmas'; something often sang about but is as rare as seeing a partridge in a pear tree, well, almost.

The *Bullring* in the city, is the great commercial and architectural attraction of Birmingham. The *Bullring* is a very large, modern shopping centre. Freddy made his way into the town centre the day after Christmas and saw that a large number of shoppers had descended on the *Bullring*, as the traditional boxing day sale was taking place. He saw these bargain hunters going about busily from store to store, triggering the security alarm frequently, as they leave the stores. There were security personnel abound, to meet the heightened need for vigilance at that time of year and checkout lines in stores snaked around the aisles. A bag - or two - or three - even more in some cases, could be seen being carried, by individual shoppers and sometimes entire families.

Meanwhile, the icy roads outside the *Bullring*, made walking a treacherous exercise. The shoppers slipped and skated, involuntarily, along what had become 'black ice'. The day was drawing to a close. With gifts and personal purchases secured, the number of shoppers dwindled towards the evening hours and the *Bullring* soon became a deserted precinct.

Freddy had a fairly good initiation into life in the *Bullring* and Birmingham remains one of the cities outside of London that he most admires. He made another visit to Birmingham another December, in the hope of seeing another 'white Christmas' but it was not to be and the atmosphere on that occasion, was just dry and cold. 'Brum' had nothing to show that resembled a 'white Christmas' that year, though he did see seven swans swimming - in a lake, and five gold rings – in a shop.

*****

North Wales was next.

The UK is a combination of four countries; England, Scotland, Northern Ireland and Wales. Freddy's understanding of the social and cultural underpinnings of the UK would not be complete without a visit to Wales. His stop in Wales was at a village called St. Asaph.

On this third leg of his country-wide tour, the

weather was typical of what everyone had come to expect of Wales. The weather was mild, with moisture in the air. Freddy had a unique taste for antiquity and the quaint, so whereas many intrepid tourists may opt for the more urban conurbations, he and his touring party, instead chose a quiet corner in the north of Wales. St. Asaph was quintessentially quaint, quiet and rustic; meeting the requirements of Freddy and his team.

Having made a few brief stops on the way, they arrived in St. Asaph and after some difficulty in navigating the route, for they had no electronic satellite navigation system, they found the accommodation. These were the days before the GPS Sat Nav. and also before Google earth maps became the answer to finding one's way around the country. This touring group will unreservedly pay homage to the little book with 'A-Z' written on the front. It got them to St. Asaph, eventually.

When the Sat Nav system began to dethrone the 'A-Z', some users of the new electronic device paid the price for being directed around by a voice in a box. Freddy had invested in one such device and found himself going around in circles in one of the busiest parts of London. The trouble with that particular Sat Nav, was that the voice came for each turning a few seconds after passing the turn. On one particular evening, Freddy was driving along a one-way street. He had a line of impatient drivers travelling behind while he was looking for Windsor Road.

"Turn left onto Windsor Road," chimed the voice from

the Sat Nav device.

At that point, he had actually gone past Windsor Road. It was a one-way street. He had to go all the way around again and make that turn onto Windsor Road, before he actually heard the command, for if he waited to hear the command from the Sat Nav, he would be late in turning again. There were countless times he had to do a double-take along roads, to hear the late commands, then go around again and do the turn from memory. Sheer agony.

Upon reaching St. Asaph in the north of Wales, Freddy and his travelling party soon settled into their 3-star accommodation. They were impressed with the front desk service, as they were greeted by a Ugandan, smartly attired in his white tunic, specifically designed to meet the hotel's requirements. This went along with his maroon-coloured trousers and brown shoes to finish off. The receptionist professionally completed the formalities at the front desk and everyone was settled in.

The surrounding area had a few houses set along the roadway, with hundreds of acres of open farm lands in between. It was their sought-after retreat on this journey, for the more serene and balmy spaces were preferred over the bustling and noisy locations. This green, open frontier of St. Asaph suited the group well.

On venturing out for a walk later that evening, Freddy and his group passed local residents, who seemed to detect that they were not locals, as symbolised by the curious turning of heads to take a second look. It was one of those small communities where everyone knows everyone else and an outsider could be spotted easily.

The morning of the second day came and they travelled down to the hub of the village, where all the basic services were available, discounting the fact that there was only one of each. As they wandered into an eatery, they were greeted with another spate of head-turning. The regulars could tell that these faces were new in the village but the travelling group had gotten used to the attention by now. Having enjoyed a meal of scrambled eggs, some mushrooms, few sausages, cups of tea and several slices of toast, they were ready to leave and carry on with their exploration.

The morning had started well but it was momentarily paralysed by the parking penalty fine they had acquired in the bay outside the café. None of them had paid attention to the parking time allowed and this fine had dampened their spirit, somewhat. With that disappointment put behind them, Freddy and company were able to make a survey of the local amenities in that St. Asaph community. In addition to the few services provided in the village, it was completed by a primary school and a single church, with a cemetery thrown in for good measure.

By mid-afternoon, they had seen and experienced St. Asaph - in its full glory. The memories of the tranquil nature of the village are everlasting. The UK, they knew, had a quieter laid-back side and they had dared themselves to find it and so, they did. Despite the limited range of services and other facilities in St. Asaph, it felt as though the village had an enviable compensation, by way of its serenity. A stop-over, tainted marginally by a traffic fine, had come to an end and it was time to leave St. Asaph behind and move on to the next stop on that road trip.

*****

Painswick was next.

The small size of St. Asaph was only rivalled by Painswick, in the Cotswold region of Gloucester. Freddy and his travelling companions made their next stop in the Cotswold and drove around until they arrived in another quintessentially quaint, quiet and rustic village which was called Painswick. A single, narrow, short street runs through Painswick. Blink whilst travelling through Painswick and you would have missed the village. Remarkably, the feel of the village was overwhelmingly personal. As Freddy and the team walked into a café, a pleasant, unspoken welcome emanated from the residents who were settled in around the small tables, having quiet talk and roast meals, with their favourite dressings. The welcome was a constant. The few business places all provided the same, friendly welcome.

Four family-friendly pubs lined the short street. They counted them. A single set of traffic lights was used to regulate the flow of traffic along that one narrow street; a street so narrow that two vehicles could not pass alongside each other. The few shops and other services extended for a few metres in two directions, from the centre of the village. Like most small villages, the social amenities were few, however, there was the unmissable church and accompanying cemetery. There was very little else.

Freddy was quite happy with his journey to *discover* the UK. He had seen several points of interest on this journey and made four key stops: Sheffield, Birmingham, St. Asaph and Painswick. The UK was more than the commercial hub of the capital and Freddy had fulfilled his personal challenge to see more. The colleagues he travelled with, shared his wish to take in a wider view of the UK. They returned to London at the end of this road trip, to face the hustle and bustle of the capital all over again.

Chapter 23

Higher Education

There were two words that helped to form a perception of the UK among scholars in the Caribbean Islands, while Freddy and his peers attended secondary school: "Cambridge" and "Oxford". Students in secondary schools studied subject content that was designed by the two leading universities in the UK. The Exam Boards of Oxford and Cambridge were on every one's lips, as they studied for their General Certificate Exams. These two cities meant everything to the students in the Caribbean Islands. The capital, London, meant less to them. So, what did Freddy and his contemporaries know about London? They knew it was the capital of the UK and heart of the commercial and economic life and that such was its popularity, that a poor boy called Dick Whittington and his cat set out on a journey to London. Or the cat must have joined him later.

Not much was known about either Cambridge or

Oxford, aside from their significance in setting exam content and awarding exam grades. The teachers of that era gave no further context of the two cities, as they had very little information at the time.

Here comes Freddy, several years later, in the New Millennium, where Cambridge would take on a new meaning. It was during the October school break, when Freddy eventually walked into the city of Cambridge, knowing that his General Certificate Exam papers were marked in this city, some years earlier. As he arrived, his first impression was formed by the River Cam, which flows through Cambridge and is visible on the approach to the colleges. Freddy's first impression was that Cambridge is a place of tranquillity and perpetuity - akin to the flowing River Cam.

Up until that point, he had no idea there were so many separate colleges and that the composite of all these separate colleges was what constituted Cambridge University and that each college has its own entrance. He also did not know that the town was primarily the university domain.

Freddy had spoken to many within the more recent Diaspora, who had visited Cambridge at some point and they shared the same misconception, that Cambridge was a large building with a main gate and that within the compound there were different buildings for each academic faculty. There were no images, at least none that Freddy and his peers had seen, of the layout of Cambridge, prior to his relocation to the UK. Though the talk was constant about exam boards, there was no verbal clarification provided for students in the

Caribbean, about Cambridge as an institution of higher learning. The reality now for Freddy, was shocking.

No one told Freddy, nor the other students in the Caribbean, that the main mode of transportation in Cambridge city centre, was the bicycle. The trusted bicycles whizzed up and down the streets outside the colleges and never before had Freddy seen so many bicycles parked in one location. Mesmerised by the uniqueness, he watched, as students collected their bicycles from where they were parked and as other students came to park theirs, in spaces vacated by the others.

With heightened curiosity and amazement, Freddy wandered through the entrance to Christ's College. Christ's College is one of about thirty colleges that make up Cambridge University and here was Freddy walking past the courts and halls, which all felt surreal. As he made his journey around the premises, a few students could be seen going about their business. The brief self-tour which he took of the college, was enlightening and as he walked back outside, he had acquired that feeling of - of something that hung in the air; erudition, he guessed. Freddy walked out knowing that he had just *trodden o'er the said same soil as ere the great scop, didst traverse;* the great scop being John Milton. Milton, the poet and Charles Darwin, the Scientist are two of the most renowned graduates of Christ's College, Cambridge.

The shops on the main road were the epitome of a period novel. They had a life and character of their own. They brought "Downton Abbey" and "Cranford" into reality. A world was unfolding in front of his eyes – he could almost touch it.

Freddy stared at the worsted sweaters that hung almost life-like on the mannequins - delicate browns and salubrious greys. Hand bags of the finest leather and creative designs were stacked on shelves, ready for the buyers. The shoes were some of the finest hand-crafted footwear that he had ever seen; patterned at the front with a double row of parallel stitching, forming the shape of a common 'm' when looking down from the wearer's position. With at best, his window shopping completed, he carried on walking along the road.

Standing by the bridge, overlooking the River Cam, was as entertaining as it was educational, for passengers were boarding the punts for a tour of the river. This was known as 'punting'. 'Punting' is a local pastime in Cambridge. The river was teeming with punts. The punt, which is a square-nosed vessel, was an attraction for tourists visiting Cambridge. Passengers were able to see a different side of the city, as they sat on these punts and were then pushed down the river by the punter with a stick. They, the drivers of the punt, braced their punt stick against the floor of the river, to gain propulsion for the vessel. They skilfully navigated the curves and turns of the river course, until passengers, punt and punter are no longer visible from the docking point at the bridge.

*****

As Freddy watched the punters, he was reminded of a similar recreational river transport, used in Jamaica. It is most well-known along the Rio Grande. There, it is called 'rafting'. This rafting on the Rio Grande, was made famous by the actor Errol Flynn and later by Ian Fleming; both of whom lived a few miles away from the Rio Grande, during the Twentieth Century. They made the exercise famous, as they were often times seen sitting on these 'rafts', made from bamboos tied together by strong cords, with a seat built on top. The driver then stood at the back and pushed it along with a rod, in a similar way to the method used by the punters on the River Cam in Cambridge.

*****

Freddy did not see Oxford but the experience of Cambridge resonated with him, as for decades, this city remained an "Exam Board" with a University. However, its wider significance and attributes were less well known to him, until he saw it first-hand and Cambridge was brought alive. The name of an exam board suddenly morphed into a teeming city where culture, history, trade and commerce flourish.

Chapter 24

Turbulent Days

London seems to be an enchanting place, chockful of character, kept alive and awake by the intricate network of buses and constant rolling of the trains; under, across, into and out of the city. What could possibly go wrong in London?

Freddy was a part of the hustle and bustle and became accustomed to the ever-present stream of tourists, with camera in hand, walking about and capturing images of well-known attractions in London. He would also see the regular flow of businessmen and diplomats, who came into the city for meetings. London was a constant buzz of activity - everything working with precision and synchronicity, like the cogs in the belly of Big Ben. However, the synchronicity of the city was disturbed, in the summer of 2005.

The seventh of July, 2005, started off as just another work day. Freddy and his colleagues were busy at their teaching posts, when news came unexpectedly, that a bomb had gone off in Central London. It was unusual to hear such a report, as life in the city flowed normally and incessantly, like the River Thames. The news was frightening, as an underground tube line was attacked. The news got worse as the bus network was also attacked. There were casualties - numbers unknown. It was still early morning in the school and thousands of commuters were in Central London, making their way to work. News came again that there was another bomb attack in Central London. There were more casualties. This was no accident and as the teachers watching the television broadcast learned more about the attacks, they became deeply worried. Before the morning was over, the worst fear was confirmed. Four bombs were detonated. Three underground tube lines and a bus were blown up and there were dozens of casualties, as a result.

The anxiety amongst Freddy and his colleagues in the staffroom, was palpable. There was stunned silence. Then, in one corner of the staffroom, Freddy noticed that a colleague, Charlotte, was in bewilderment and distress beyond their level of dismay. Charlotte was being consoled by Alison, who was her close friend and colleague. What he heard next summed up Charlotte's pain.

"I am calling my son and he is not answering," Charlotte explained, between her tears.
This was painful for Charlotte, much more than it was for her colleagues.

"He has probably turned it off," replied Alison

reassuringly.

"He should be ringing to let me know that he is ok," said a disconcerted Charlotte, "I know for sure that he has his phone, I saw him using it this morning, when I dropped him off at the station."

More colleagues gathered and shared their concern, as this was turning out to be a dark day for everyone. Midday was approaching and still no word from Charlotte's son. More confirmation came from the television news in the staffroom, that the bombings were not accidental but were deliberately carried out by a group of men known to the police. The casualty toll rose with each bulletin. Freddy's workplace was unsettled. London was unsettled.

London had been unsettled by demonstrations and protests in the past. On those occasions, the participants in the disturbance are always visible to everyone, as protestors openly venting their displeasure for all to see. Here now, it was different. It was worrying to all, as the participants in the bomb attacks were invisible, hidden among the people. Everyone felt vulnerable.

Charlotte's worry mounted, as the day dragged on. Her son had not called. As they watched the television bulletin, the reality became more numbing, as the horrific images of injured passengers flashed across the screen. The ripped clothing, bloodied faces, broken limbs and burnt skin of the victims, shocked the already terrified public to the point of repulsion.

"I believe my son is caught up in all this, his phone has stopped ringing," concluded Charlotte, as she watched the chilling reports on the television.

A television was hung in the far corner of the staffroom, above the staff lockers, so that staff who had a break or who were taking lunch, could see news updates.

Charlotte's son had taken the underground tube in the morning, on one of those lines where the underground tube trains were attacked. He has used the same route for the past ten months and his mother has always been able to contact him and get a reply, whether by voice or text; today, there was nothing. The worry intensified, as it was now past midday. Her attempts to reach him by phone proved unsuccessful and she had no other means of contacting him now, as he was not going to be at work. Time was going fast and as it did, Charlotte's resolve waned.

As Charlotte sat in a daze, Kerry, the secretary, walked in with a message from the principal.

"The principal has sent me to get you," said Kerry. The others wondered what that was about. They feared the worst had happened and bad news about her son, had reached the school.

"I believe he is going to send you home early," Kerry said.

They all breathe a collective sigh of relief. Charlotte went off with Kerry, leaving the others in apprehension as to what could have happened to her son. The television updates were coming fast, as more details were available to the police. The image of a makeshift treatment centre on the street, close to one of the targeted train stations, was further evidence of the severity of the crisis. The city was beset by panic. This was a real emergency. Volunteer workers got involved in the recovery effort and phone lines were set up for anyone concerned about a family member or friend, to call for information. As with most instances of panic and confusion, false information started springing up from unknown sources. There were rumours of another attack, at a neighbouring station, in North London. This turned out to be no more than a rumour arising from the abounding chaos and confusion.

Charlotte was sent home in understandable grief. Freddy and the other staff members got no further updates from her about her son. Fortunately for them at work, no one else reported anyone missing, or had family who may have been caught up in the carnage. They left work that afternoon, deeply concerned about Charlotte, as her son who had not been in contact with her.

Later that afternoon, at around 4:45pm, staff received the news about Charlotte's son. The school's deputy headteacher had sent a text around to inform them, as he knew that all staff were aware of Charlotte's anguish. To this day, Freddy can still remember the moment he read those words from the text.

"Dear all, I have just heard from Charlotte who is still trying to come to terms with what happened today. Unfortunately, her son's phone battery had died. He is now home, safe and sound."

Charlotte's colleagues were relieved. This was one of those days when the city was in collective shock but managed to show resolve. The magic and intrigue of the city of London was disturbed on that day. Over fifty people had died, as a result of the bombings.

This was not the only disruption to the orderly nature of the city, that Freddy experienced in London. Yet, none had been so horrific as these bombings; causing mass death, physical and emotional life-changing impact, for scores of people.

There was a protest in 2010 which was triggered by an increase in university fees by the government and hundreds of protestors descended on the streets of central London. As the throng of protestors paraded around the main thoroughfares in the business and commercial heart of London, the police could be seen kettling the discontented crowd. 'Kettling' is a method whereby, the police form a semi-circle across the path of the protestors to restrict their movement.

Unfortunately for Freddy, he was caught up in that university fee protest of December 2010. The scene was overwhelming as amidst the protestors, there were many who were engaged in burning of public infrastructure and looting. Others among the crowd, displayed violent behaviour, which resulted in serious injury to many. The police made several arrests.

As Freddy and other commuters hurried to get out of the melee, he caught glimpses of police officers on horses, kitted out in riot gear and high visibility vests. In front of them were hundreds of demonstrators, shouting slogans which could not be decrypted from the distance where Freddy was, as he tried to find available transport, to get home. The events of that cold December day still linger in his mind.

The Millennial migrants, such as Freddy, have seen

the quiet streets of the city become cacophonous on a few other occasions. Trade Union matters, employment issues and disagreements with government decisions, have caused protests in the city, time after time.

Freddy was unable to speak of disruptions to the routine of life in London, which occurred in the Twentieth Century. He heard of the *Brixton riot* and read reports but had no direct experience of it. However, in August 2011, he experienced the aftermath of a riot.

The unrest in August 2011, stemmed from the shooting of a black British man by the police, under questionable circumstances, in Tottenham Hale. Friends and family of the deceased, demonstrated outside the local police station to show their dissatisfaction with the way information was given to the victim's family, by the police. The absence of information from the authorities, led to the confrontation which triggered the full-scale riot.

As it turned out, Freddy had gone past the Tottenham area an hour or two before things turned upside down and things literally were, turned upside down.

Sitting at home later that Saturday night, Freddy saw the frightening scenes of a fire that was raging less than a mile away, on Tottenham high road. The news story confirmed what the images were about and he feared that the situation was likely to get worse. The vision of burning police cars was reminiscent of scenes from "*Judgement Day*", the movie which showed scenes of inferno-like flames engulfing what once served as symbols of modernity. Carnage and chaos reigned on the high road.

The news broadcast was continuous. The situation became more intense and what had started in the vicinity of the Tottenham police station, was swiftly spreading to several areas of London and some other cities in the UK. Buildings were torched. More cars were burned. Bewildered, yet courageous firefighters fought feverishly to douse the flames that danced beneath the plumes of smoke, escaping from the burning buildings.

Freddy ventured onto the road a few days later, when the dust had settled and when the flames had died down and tried to figure out where certain shops were, but he could not. The high road was a shadow of itself. The affected shops had become heaps of badly burnt bricks, twisted steel, broken pieces of glass and charred wood. There was rubble everywhere. Tottenham high road had been the epicentre of the devastation. As Freddy walked along, the smell of burnt material lingered in the atmosphere and clung to his nostrils. Inhalation of the putrid air made his breathing laboured and arduous.

Freddy carried on walking and the tale was the same along that high road, where the evidence of destruction continuously greeted him. The street was burnt to a dark hue. There were dried blackened water-marks, forming horrid abstract shapes along the street, left behind from the work of firefighters, who battled the fires that had been set to vehicles. In some spots, Freddy could see tiny cremated particles of plastic, that once formed the casing of batteries and dashboards, strewn on the fire-burnt road. There were wires from tyres of cars, thin metal strips from doorframes and glove compartments, now lining the spots where cars were parked, a few days before.

Some shops on the high road and in the nearby retail park, had not been burnt. However, they were looted. Freddy extended his reconnaissance walk to the Tottenham retail park and saw the large sheets of ply board that covered the entrances and windows of most shops. This, the owners did, either after the store was looted, or as a precaution against looting. He noticed that the stores that were already looted in the retail park, were those trading in high end consumables. Stores with fashionable clothing, jewellery, expensive trainers, mobile phones, computers and household appliances, bore the brunt of the looting. The sight of cardboard boxes in front of some stores, indicated that some looters had removed items from the packaging, perhaps in checking for aesthetic quality of the loot or as a means of reducing the weight of the goods. Plastic wrapping, binding cords and isolated items of clothing, littered the forecourt of the retail park.

In the ensuing months, the list of people taken before the courts across London and charged for looting, included a range of ethnic groups from different parts of the city and beyond its boundary.

The effects of the bombings in July 2005 and the days following the university fee protest in December 2010 and the London riot of August 2011, demonstrate that despite the multi-ethnic composition of the UK in general and London in particular, there is always a desire to restore the country to normalcy after a crisis.

These turbulent days do not last forever.

Chapter 25

The Diaspora at Work

Nearly two decades after Freddy had arrived in the UK, he had seen enough to know that the Caribbean Diaspora, particularly Jamaicans, have played a central role in helping to shape the economic and social landscape of Great Britain. With the Brixton riot and the Tottenham riot aside, which the Caribbean Diaspora have been linked to, there is continued service of the Diaspora, to the preservation of the British way of life.

Freddy knew that the pioneers who travelled to the UK, were instrumental in filling job vacancies that contributed to the reconstruction of Great Britain, after World War 2. Further to that, they undertook jobs, such as caring for the sick and the elderly and also provided labour-force in factories. While Freddy was not around to see this taking place, he had been reliably informed about the work of his predecessors. The Jamaican

Diaspora as he was told, mostly worked in the transport industry. There were few bus drivers among them, however, the Jamaicans in the London transport network, mainly worked as conductors. Freddy, nearly twenty years after arriving in Great Britain, in the new Millennium, no longer sees the bus conductors.

The era of the bus conductors came to an end, early in the New Millennium. He merely saw a few 'clippies', by the time he arrived in the UK. Female conductors were endearingly nicknamed, 'clippies'. It was a new time and a new politics - a new kind of management plan called 'downsizing'. Many cost-cutting measures were tested by the government, such as making the bus conductors redundant. Conductors then, used a portable ticket machine, which was slung from the shoulder and was operated by winding up the attached handle. A strip of paper was then ejected with the details of the transaction and that would be given to the paying passenger, as proof of payment.

The conductors collected the fares on these old Routemaster buses. With one transaction completed, the conductor, in all his or her dexterity, would roll out the next ticket for the next passenger, collect the fare and issue the ticket – all in one fell swoop.

The Millennial thinking brought in a new bus design that had no need for a conductor, as the entrance was at the front, opposite the driver. The driver was now able to see the oncoming passengers and sell tickets to the them, at the same time.

"Health and Safety" was another reason for the end of the Routemaster days, as passengers were at risk of falling, as they hopped on and off those buses. When the Routemaster buses were made redundant, the need for conductors became redundant.

The drivers on the new buses, operated as driver and conductor. From his seat, the driver needed to turn his head to the left so that he faces the oncoming passengers. Operating the cash pan, meant that he was turning his head forty-five degrees to the left - for the steering wheel is on the right.

*****

Having travelled to Spain on holiday, Freddy was to learn that the UK is one of a minority of countries, where vehicles drive on the left of the road and vehicles predominately have the driver's seat on the right-hand side of the vehicle. He was teased by a friend in Spain about the British driving on the wrong side of the road, while most of the European countries drove on the right side of the road.

*****

Someone must have complained about the position of the ticket printer in the new buses, as newer models of London buses have the ticket printer at a more convenient angle for the driver. The ticket printer was later replaced with an oyster card reader and Freddy had his first encounter with the new system, on a route 259 bus from Manor House Station going towards Kings Cross, St. Pancras.

On a busy London day, the journey into the city centre requires patience and resilience, as it is common to be badly delayed due to the volume of traffic heading into the city.

At last, the number 259 bus arrived at Freddy's stop. Passengers boarding the bus used the front entrance opposite the driver, as the other opening towards the middle of the left panel, was for exit. He stepped on behind a couple. The man was attired in a skull cap, and a loose-fitting, cream-coloured shirt with loose, baggy trousers of the same colour and texture, wearing dark-coloured sandals upon his feet. Alongside him, the woman was adorned in a light blue headscarf, wrapped loosely about the head and shoulders with the ends left to dangle freely down the back. Her adornment was completed with darker blue loosely-fitting blouse and similar loosely-fitting, baggy trousers.

Freddy entered the doorway behind them, as queuing was the orderly way to board the buses. He watched the couple in front curiously and studied their every move. They were about mid-forties in age. Whatever they did, he would do, as it was his first bus ride using the new oyster card. The card, which is the same size as a regular bank card or telephone calling card, has the logo of London Transport emblazoned on it. His was blue in colour. To make it ready for use on the buses, the oyster card must be topped up by a local shop keeper, or by a clerk at the train station.

At these retail points, a card reader is positioned on the counter. Upon a request for 'top up', the card is placed on the reader, any side down. The required amount of money is then entered into the computer connected to the reader or electronic till, by the operator. The amount is then programmed into the card and it is ready for use. A passenger may buy the corresponding amount for a day, a week or a month's worth of bus travel.

With oyster card in hand and eyes glued on the couple, Freddy moved onto the bus. The man placed the oyster card on a reader that was built into the bus, at a convenient angle to the left of the driver's line of sight. There was a sound. '*Be be beep*'. He walked down the passage. The woman touched her oyster card on the reader and followed her companion down the passage. Having seen the technique, which was fairly straightforward, Freddy did the same and got his confirmation that his fare was paid via the '*Be-be beep,*' response from the card reader. Freddy walked down the passage of the bus, feeling pleased with himself and sat down next to a window. He was on his way to Kings Cross St. Pancras.

*****

The work of the Diaspora has not stopped and a

Jamaican migrant, or a descendant of a Jamaican migrant, can be seen driving a bus in many parts of London. The Caribbean Diaspora have continued to work in the Health sector, as nurses and health care assistants. Freddy has spent some time around some of these proud workers, who have told him that they enrolled in nurse training and achieved their qualifications in Great Britain. As he discovered during his years in the UK, there is hardly a hospital in London without a health worker; be it a doctor, nurse, nurse's assistant or phlebotomist, who is not from the African or Caribbean Diaspora.

The presence of the Caribbean Diaspora in the UK, means more than riot. The honest and hard work done by Caribbean migrants, supersedes the incidents of disruption and damage linked to the Diaspora. A care home, especially in London, is hardly complete without an African or Caribbean health worker, who is always dutifully attired in pin-striped top of pink or blue and navy-blue trousers – selflessly getting on with the task from day to day. Who could disagree that the work of the many dedicated hard-working migrants is of great value to Great Britain? Who could disagree that the Caribbean Diaspora make a profound impact on the British way of life, in one form or another.

The Millennial migrants, such as Freddy, arrived in Great Britain to see members of the Caribbean Diaspora working in government. The second generation of the early migrants have become Members of the British Parliament – a thought which no one had, when the first ship arrived in 1948. Some Jamaicans have had very influential jobs in the British legal system, as lawyers and others as immigration personnel.

*****

When Freddy arrived in the UK, the Jamaican Diaspora was tainted in some ways, by the perception of Jamaicans as 'Yardies'. The term was conscripted from the local *lingua* of the Jamaicans in the UK. 'Yard' was the term used by Jamaicans, to affectionately refer to Jamaica. 'Yardie' was the derivative of the word 'Yard', used initially by Jamaicans to claim their allegiance to their original homeland of Jamaica.

The use of the term has, however, become a metaphor for Jamaicans who have been involved in illicit activities in the UK. This was widely used by the British law enforcement, who sometimes extend it to "Yardie gangs". The reference to all Jamaicans abroad therefore, as "Yardies", is no longer politically correct, as that label has taken on a negative connotation. A Jamaican is a self-respecting, law-abiding, hard-working individual who gives of his or her time and experiences for the wellbeing of others.

*****

The work of the Diaspora goes beyond health care,

politics, law and transport. The delivery service sector could not have been the same without the Caribbean Diaspora. Freddy once got home to find a note stating that his parcel could not be delivered, as a signature was needed. The note went on to say that the parcel would be delivered the next day, between 9am and 2pm. His first reaction was one of confusion.

"Why would the delivery driver come back the following day between the same hours during a work week?" Freddy asked himself.

He stood staring at the note, quizzically.

"If no one was home in the day, during the time of the first attempted delivery, what are the chances that someone will be home between the same times the next day?" he mused.

On this particular afternoon, he decided to give the delivery man a call, as a mobile number was written on the note.

"Hello, this is Everton, can I help?" said the voice at the other end of the phone.

"Good evening," said Freddy, "I just came home and picked up a note saying you didn't get to leave my parcel and that you will come back tomorrow..."

By that point, Freddy was cut short. As far as the delivery man was concerned, Freddy was beating about the bush. The delivery man already knew what the call was about and he needed to settle the matter quickly; he had more parcels to deliver before night-fall.

"What's you name sar?" he asked, interrupting Freddy's detailed explanation.

Detecting a familiar intonation in the delivery man's

voice, Freddy concluded that he had a connection with the Jamaican Diaspora. Deciding there on the spot that it could best serve his interest, if the delivery man knew that he, himself was also of the Jamaican Diaspora, Freddy then replied in a similar intonation. He told the delivery man his name and address.

"Oh yes man, I done drop yuh side long time," he replied, "I comin back tomorro same time."

"That won't help me, I will be at work and nobody will be home," Freddy told him.

"aw'right, tell me a time an' I will push back your delivery till after work."

"I will try to get home by 4:30, so any time after that is good." Freddy said.

"Cool, look fo' me round 5-ish,"

"Give thanks, I will see you then," Freddy stated.
Everton kept to his promise. At around 5:20 the next day, Freddy heard the sound of his door bell. Running downstairs and opening the door, he saw the delivery man, parcel in one hand and an electronic tablet in the other hand, with an attached pen dangling, suspended by a swirly cord of about a foot in length. After confirming his identity, he instructed Freddy to sign on the glass protected section of the tablet, where there was the space for signature. With the formalities over, they had a brief chat.

"I just av five more o' these parcels to drop fo' tonight," Everton said in a tone of accomplishment and satisfaction with his day's work.
By this time, he had told Freddy his name and confirmed that he is a Jamaican.

"Oh, well that is good," Freddy assured him, "you can get some early sleep tonight man."

"Yes, it is how the job is sometimes - you get a good day and sometimes you get a very bad day, but I not complainin', I get used to it," Everton explained, "doin' this job fo' fifteen years now," he added. "From I been in Inglan, I been workin day and sometimes night. This country tough, an' I av children going to school so I av to work," he said.

Freddy had become a mere listener in the conversation, as Everton made good use of the opportunity to relate his work history, dedication to duty and personal life to Freddy. Who could blame him for sharing his success story?

"Between ma wife an' maself, we try to give the children a good education, so they can av a good future," concluded Everton, at long last.

Another minute or so later and Everton had left. He left to complete his round for the day. Freddy could take many interpretations from Everton's disclosure; however, he knew that Everton is a representation of the Jamaican Diaspora. who dedicate themselves to hard work. Everton shows, like so many other men from the Diaspora, that he cares for his family and their wellbeing and he is prepared to work hard to provide for them. Freddy was mindful that there is substantial literature that speak of fathers who do little for their children but scarcely any mention of the 'Evertons' from Jamaica.

Everton is not in isolation. He is a migrant. He is a family man and a dedicated worker. He is a member of the Caribbean Diaspora; whose work helps to keep the British way of life revolving. Riots aside, these are the workers who help to make the Service industry, the Health sector, Education and the Construction industry, what they are.

Chapter 26

Nostalgia

Not much has changed since the time that the *Empire Windrush* landed at Tilbury docks, in the south east of the UK. The emotions were rife, raw even, for some who may have left very young children and ageing family behind. From the time the early migrants came, they had plans. These plans mainly fit into one of three categories.

Firstly, there were those who planned to spend between two and five years, save enough money and go back to the Caribbean and live comfortably. However, that turned out to be an aspirational, rather than a realistic timeline. The reality was that no one knew the length of time that would be needed to save enough money to return and live comfortably. What would a weekly family or single-living budget look like? That dream of two to five years return, soon faded and in many cases, it was extended to ten years.

Secondly, there was a group that had a plan of five or more years. However, just as the group with the two to five-year timeline, they soon realised that it was not economically realistic. Thirdly, there were those who planned to stay in the UK until retirement, then return to the Caribbean. As it turned out, the four hundred and ninety-two arrivals had quite different outcomes. Some returned a few years later, without achieving their economic objectives. Some stayed for many years and retired back to the Caribbean. Others remained, to be part of the founding fabric of the Diaspora in the UK.

This is significant, as the next generation born in the UK, would continue to change Great Britain into the multicultural nexus it is today. They have never severed ties with the homeland. The nostalgia has always been there. Some members of that early group of migrants, have travelled back to the homeland to visit friends and family. Some have left it for one grand 'return home' trip. Others plan the trip every year (for many years) but have not been able to make it a reality. The reasons vary but one, most tragic of all the stories, is one Freddy recently heard of; the details of which, had he not heard of it from a trustworthy contact, would be thought to be a purely made up script.

Donald was in his teen years when the *Empire Windrush* sailed away from the Caribbean. Georgie, his older cousin and mentor, started to consider the trip to Great Britain, as the pioneers became settled and news of Great Britain began to filter back home. Some of the news was not of the most pleasant nature, however, on the whole, it was beginning to interest more and more

Jamaicans. Georgie made the decision that he would travel to the UK. Needless to say, Donald was to accompany him; he trusted his older cousin to make good decisions.

A few years went by. They worked. They saved some money. With the required money for travel now available, they made final plans, packed their bags and set sail for the UK. Like many before, they had difficulty finding accommodation, initially. Eventually, they met other countrymen and soon found their footing. Almost everyone who migrated in those years can attest to the experience of having difficulty with accommodation, upon arrival in the UK. This was the story of the intrepid migrant.

The cousins would soon find work separately. The big new world was now their oyster. Donald had a different expectation of his time in the UK. For him, it was a young man's dream come true. He had a few job changes. He was not known to remain for too long in any one job. Things were different at the time; jobs were plenty. The war had ended nearly a decade before but there were still many vacancies to be filled. Distribution companies, hospitals, rail companies and factories, all needed new hands. Donald had no problem finding work.

Georgie had other plans for his time in the UK. His wife was left back at home and he intended to get her to join him in the UK, as soon as possible. This might explain why Georgie kept his jobs for longer periods. All the time, he remained a mentor for Donald. The relationship remained after Georgie's wife arrived and the relationship remained after the first child was born to Georgie and his wife. It was clear that these two cousins were loyal to one another and nothing would separate them. By the time the third child was born to Georgie and his wife, Donald was already twice a godfather.

So, the years rolled on by and Georgie would make several trips to see family and friends back in the Caribbean. After each trip, he would return to his home in Essex. On each occasion, he encouraged Donald to accompany him. Twenty years went by and Donald had not made the trip. There was hope yet. He would go soon. Thirty years went by and things remained the same. More serious plans were made and everyone connected to the cousins was hopeful that the time was coming soon. Everyone was imagining Donald heading to the airport for his trip but the wait dragged on and the anticipation continued to build up.

During these years, the early migrants were establishing themselves in the UK. Dreams were becoming reality. Many were going back to their original communities in the Caribbean after ten years; sticking to their original plan. Others were retiring and moving back to reside, as initially intended. At the same time, those who intended to remain in the UK were retiring yearly and making the UK home - for good.

A total of forty years went by and despite numerous trips by Georgie, who had made the UK his permanent home, Donald was still to fulfil that ambition of travelling back to visit friends and family. These were now retirement years and things needed to be done sooner rather than later - well, sooner was no longer an option. There were numerous family occasions and with each passing year, the question would arise about his return date.

"When are you going to visit the Caribbean, 'D'?" someone would ask.

"I am going, I just need to get myself ready for the trip," he would reply.

"But you said that last time we met 'D', are you serious this time that you will be going?"

"I am hopeful, very hopeful. Look out, I am going to surprise you one of these days," he would reply.

This went on for fifty years. Fifty years later and 'D' had not made that return trip. The plan had become more robust. All the stops had been pulled out and the date was set. 'D' was going to return to his native home in the Caribbean, albeit, more than fifty years later. 'D' was going to return for good. From a trip to visit, the deliberation eventually became a retirement plan. Everything was set and personal belongings were packaged and sent by ship. Incidentally, it was the route by which he had come but while his possessions were shipped, he would travel by air.

At long last, Donald would make his trip, accompanied by Georgie and two other friends who had once shared a flat with Georgie and Donald. The two friends, Ishmael and Egbert, had settled in the UK. Ishmael was accompanied by his two grandchildren, a boy, 17 and a girl, 14. He was taking them on their first holiday to the Caribbean and they had planned their holiday to coincide with Donald's return. They left

London Gatwick airport in high spirits. This was going to be some homecoming for Donald. The group of friends and family touched down nine hours later at Kingston, Norman Manley International airport.

At the funeral two weeks later, Georgie, Ishmael and Egbert could only reminisce on their time spent over the years with Donald. Donald had died four days after arriving back in Portland, Jamaica. The doctors declared 'natural cause' as the reason for his death.

This is one of many stories where nostalgia had beset the Caribbean Diaspora in the UK. In the New Millennium, however, the nostalgia of home was relieved by technological advancements. The mobile phone became a lifestyle-changing gadget. Initially, it was fashionable to own a mobile phone; it was even a sign of prestige for some. From the days of the large box-like device, with an attached battery, the modern-day, sleek design of mobile phones made them much less conspicuous. As more and more people use the mobile phone, it has evolved into a useful piece of new-age paraphernalia, making social, business and domestic life easier.

All the Diaspora groups in the UK make good use of mobile phones in communicating with friends and family in their country of origin and the Caribbean Diaspora are well involved in this. It was common for a call to be made back to friends overseas from anywhere, while on the go. The feeling of homesickness can disappear via a phone call to a mobile phone in the Caribbean. Things got even better, as video calling apps have made instant face to face connections to the

Islands of the Caribbean, a possibility.

For those in the Diaspora who are unable to travel back to the Caribbean frequently, the mobile phone is a welcome piece of gear. The computer also helps with the alleviation of 'homesickness', as an email to a family member overseas gets to them more quickly than a letter by post. Twenty-first Century methods of keeping in touch, have reduced the distress of nostalgia. With new technology, the Caribbean Diaspora in the UK can get in touch with others, with the press of a button.

Direct communication with family in the UK, is now a pleasurable, private and necessary pastime. Almost every family member in the Caribbean has access to a mobile phone. However, the one regret that the Diaspora may have with regards to the mobile phone, is the familiar message that appears from time to time, from contacts in the Caribbean: ***"Send me some credit nuh."***

Chapter 27

Meeting the Hemingways

"Fancy a game of tennis?" Alan asked Freddy.

"Yes, I haven't played in a while though," Freddy replied. Alan was a friend he had met some years before. They kept in contact and had been friends ever since. Freddy had followed Alan to a few tea parties and he had been a guest at a few events that Freddy has been invited to.

"Haven't played in a while myself, so don't worry about it, I will be at the court at Becketts Park at 2pm," he told Freddy.

"I just have to take Juliet for a doctor's appointment and I will meet you there," Freddy explained.

"Oh, is your wife ok?" he inquired, "give her my regards."

"Yes, Juliet is fine, just a routine appointment."

*****

Freddy first met Alan on a train, while travelling back to London from Manchester. Sitting there in a forward-facing seat, with his feet stretched out under the table serving his seat and the seat facing him, he was absorbed in a story on the front page of the newspaper. Having bought the paper outside Manchester Piccadilly station moments before boarding the train, Freddy was deeply focused on the details of the story, when a travelling party came to jolt him back to the reality of his surroundings.

"These are our seats, D26, D27, D28, D30," said a voice that he guessed to be a girl of around fourteen years old.

"Look, there is enough space for the bags, over there," another voice chimed. The speaker, Freddy guessed must be around eight or nine years old. It was a boy.

Freddy was sitting in D25, '25' was his favourite number and he was lucky to have been assigned seat '25' when he booked his ticket for travel. This was a fast train, operated by a company known for its good service and comfortable journeys up and down the UK. This service was usually fully booked. As the seat next to him and those opposite, had been marked **"Reserved",** Freddy knew that it was only a matter of time while the passengers were boarding, before he would have company - indeed, loads of company.

"Hi, I'm Alan, this is my wife Kirsty, my daughter

Emily and my son Jack," said the man who was with the group of four. Freddy returned the greeting and introduction. That was the beginning of a long enduring friendship between himself and the Hemingway family. A train journey was all it took. Alan seemed to be a good talker and Freddy was known to have his way with a few words, whenever he was in the mood.

Alan and Freddy chatted about the seasons, sport, the government - a very spirited discourse on that - and performing arts, history and travel. His children found different ways to pass the time and they occasionally ate sandwiches from their snack pack. Emily was engrossed in music, as she listened through her headset. Meanwhile, Jack was busy pressing buttons on a gadget that he held with both hands and worked his thumbs mostly, relentlessly, on the key pad for most of the journey. Kirsty buried her attention in a novel, on the cover was written: 'From Light into a Brighter Light – Retold'. It must have interested her deeply, as she kept reading for at least an hour and a half, without a break.

So deeply engaged in their activities were they, that when the refreshment trolley rolled by, no one except Alan and Freddy, had the desire for refreshment. He had a coffee while Freddy had tea. Belatedly, Kirsty, looking over her shoulder as the trolley went by, called out to the sales attendant to get his attention. She, perhaps on second thought, had decided that a pack of crisps and a cup of tea, may be a fitting complement to her reading. She bought tea. She had a few sips of the tea. It was left to stand on the table in the cup until presumably, it got too cold to be tasty. A taste presumably, that would have disturbed the palate and maybe the appetite for the book.

Freddy found out then, that Alan was a dedicated sport fan. He liked volleyball, tennis and cycling. Cricket he realised, Alan did not like, no way - he loved it! They had a few things in common he thought. As they chatted, Alan mentioned swimming. A part of that conversation elicited information from Freddy about his swimming exploits. They were non-existent.

"I don't swim," Freddy told him.

"But you told me that you lived in the Caribbean, there is water all around the Islands," Alan reminded Freddy.

"That's true but the reality is that only a very small percentage of the Islanders can swim," Freddy said, in a bid to dispel the myth and misconception about all those fantastic swimmers from the Caribbean.

It has been a foregone conclusion of many Britons with whom Freddy came into contact, that everyone from the Caribbean Islands can swim. That is so far from the reality. There were other misconceptions that Freddy had to clarify for Alan. Alan was also of the opinion that the Islands, especially Jamaica, have 'Rastas' on every street corner and highway. He was quite mystified when Freddy explained that he could spend a day travelling around Jamaica, in particular and only run into a few Rastafarians. While they form a part of the local culture and religion, the percentage of the total population is not as staggeringly high as generally believed, considering that the Island has approximately 3 million residents.

*****

Rastafarianism originated in Jamaica in the 1930s, as a religion with 'Jah' being the central God. The religion was promoted by different nationalists, such as Marcus Garvey, who had a 'movement' for taking black nationals back to Africa. Ethiopia is cited as the main destination or *'The Promised Land'*. The religion has several tenets, such as living naturally, consuming fruits, ground provisions and vegetables, as part of the 'ital' diet. The religion also believes in growing the hair upon the head into dreadlocks and the smoking of marijuana, is one of the principles of the worship.

Rastafarianism has spread internationally and there are currently over 700,000 Rastafarians across the world. Rastafarianism gained popularity, mainly by touring reggae music bands, especially in the 1970s and 1980s. The reggae music bands were formed by Rastafarian singers and players of instruments. Some of the famous bands and performers are 'Burning Spear', 'Israel Vibration', 'The Mighty Diamonds', 'The Wailers' and 'Black Uhuru'.

The Rastafarian religion is well developed in the UK and other European countries, such as The Netherlands and Germany. It is also significant in African countries, such as Democratic Republic of Congo, South Africa and Malawi. A Rastafarian may be of the House of Nyahbinghi, Twelve Tribes of Israel or

Bobo Ashanti.

*****

The conversation between Freddy and Alan went on with a range of topics being explored and numerous points of view exchanged. This would have continued but the announcement was made that the train would soon be arriving at London Euston station - their final stop. Arriving at London Euston on a train from Manchester, or from any other city in the UK, means a frantic dash to get off the train and out onto the platform. Then everyone is funnelled through the barriers, out the gates and into the open court. Fully aware of this, Freddy and Alan made sure to exchange phone numbers before getting off the train. They just had to carry on their conversation at some point in the future.

******

"Alright then, see you at Becketts Park, after you have taken Juliet for her appointment," Alan concluded, "I have some other friends joining us today, so see you at 2pm."

The weather was good so Alan, with his friends, Steve, Andy and Tom were able to get their game going.

Freddy joined them afterwards. They played for the better part of the afternoon as the weather permitted and made a plan to go back the following week.

Freddy's friendship with the Hemingway family went beyond the tennis court. They had been out together on day trips and cycling exploits around Broxbourne cycle course but by attending dinner parties with the Hemingways, he saw another aspect of the Britain culture.

At one dinner party he attended with Alan and his family, Freddy was seeing first-hand, some of what constitutes "The British way of Life". It is a term that has made its rounds in parliament, on the news channels and on social media, still no one has made a clear definition of its meaning. However, judging by its context, Freddy believed that the nature of this dinner party, was part of it.

Outside the house, in the back garden were seven wooden combi table and chair units, much like the ones seen outside cafés and pubs around the UK. Each unit could seat six guests. Various drinks were laid out on each table, accompanied by a flat tray of muffins, scones, tubs of jam and tubs of cream. Cutlery was laid out, alongside the snacks. The guests poured in on time. On time. There is something called "Caribbean time" that crossed Freddy's mind, as he sat there and noted that the seats were fully occupied by the guests - on time.

The settled guests were soon ushered by the host, table by table, to the serving area outside the conservatory, for their main meal. Each guest was given a plate and napkin and instructed to help themselves to mini samosas. Next, there was a person serving skewers with portions of diced chicken, separated with alternating cubes of sweet peppers. The next person was serving cuts of meat and poultry and this was followed by the serving of potatoes. There was a choice of mashed or roast potatoes. The serving line was complete with burgers, as an addition, or as an alternative option to the meat and potatoes. As expected, the burgers were the predominant choice of the children. To finish, two bowls of salad were at the end of the table, containing lettuce, tomatoes, sweetcorn and olives, topped off with salad dressing.

The food choice, in some ways, was a culinary cultural contrast to a typical Caribbean menu, which would include containers of rice and peas with gravy, baked or barbequed chicken, coleslaw, possibly some pork and in some cases, a selection of yams and dumplins, to complete the line-up.

However, Freddy was prepared to enjoy this more Eurocentric cuisine and relish the difference, as any food connoisseur would do. His eclectic taste had endeared him to appreciate cultural foods from Africa, South America, Asia minor, Europe, The Far East and The Middle East.

With the serving completed and dining going well, conversations were buzzing. The range of topics included holiday, travel and work issues, by one group of women and cooking skills and fitness, by another group. Then there were discussions about the *Ashes*, mainly by the men. Freddy soon realised that he was jettisoned amongst cricket fans, who like Alan, did not like the game but loved it. The *Ashes* urn is a symbolic trophy, commemorating a series between England and Australia, in 1882. The competition for the *Ashes*, remains as a cricketing rivalry between Australia and England. It generates a tense contention between the two countries, as winning the trophy symbolises cricket supremacy between two long-standing commonwealth cricketing countries.

"We will take back the *Ashes*, no doubt about it," declared Mike, "the Aussie boys won't know what hit them this time."

Mike was a guest at the dinner party, who was not just a pundit but had actually played some first-class cricket, at county level.

"The Aussie bowling attack is weak, since Shane Warne and Brett Lee left the team," added Nick.

Nick was Alan's boyhood friend.

"Our team is at full strength this year. Alastair Cook is a runs machine and there are some new good players around him," Mike continued, "we are definitely going to give them a *whitewash*."

Freddy wondered how long it would take for Alan to join in the discussion. Alan certainly likes to get his point across, so it was only a matter of time before he joined in to help *rubbish* the Aussies. He soon set about laying down the batting line up that England needed to use and how the bowling attack should be marshalled. He predicted a similar score line as Mike - a series sweep. Most of them had already made plans to be at Lord's Cricket Ground when the tournament arrives there.

The afternoon was rounded off with tea. A cup of tea was close to hand at most social or formal gathering of friends or associates, in the UK. This therefore might be said to be a part of "The British way of Life".

It is nearly impossible to fully explore the range of features that constitute the hallmark of the English 'culture'; a culture which is still to be finitely worded. However, who would argue against the British National Ploughing Championship, the full English breakfast and an antique auction, as some of the defining cultural features of the UK? Then there is the motor car auction.

The motor car auction was one of those lively expressions of commercial life that Freddy saw, in the UK. The fleet of cars at an auction can range from vintage automobiles that have been retired long ago, to cars and other vehicles of a few months in age. Crowds turn up at every staging of these auctions and take their place in the pit - rows of seats arranged in a fashion similar to seats in an arena - except this goes across from left to right instead of all the way around. This arrangement of the sales floor, allows the cars to be driven through the gap between the audience and the auctioneer.

The cars are driven into the enclosed area and the engine is switched off before the auctioneer. He takes obvious delight in giving his pitch, which is based on the beauty or the internal features of the vehicle. There is atmosphere. Everyone awaits the auctioneer's pitch. Freddy listens intently.

"Lovely blue Toyota car. Only done 50, 000 miles.

The Man Who Came to London

Genuine miles. One owner from new. Beautiful paintwork. Starting bid at one thousand. One thousand once, one thousand twenty-five, one thousand fifty, one thousand seventy-five," the auctioneer heralds.

He adds more precision to his descriptions, before carrying on with his pitch.

"Very efficient on fuel. Bucket seats. One thousand seventy-five once, twice…"

Before the gavel comes down, a potential buyer raises a hand, pushing the bid higher.

"Two thousand. Two thousand once, twice…"

This went on for a while until there were no more hands being raised. The car was eventually sold to the highest bidder.

These are some of the outings that Freddy and the Hemingways attended together. Although these events are not unique to the UK and are carried out in many countries, there is a feeling somehow, that they have an origin in the UK and were then filtered around the world. Cricket is believed to have been invented by the English. Nowadays, the game is played in over one hundred and twenty-five countries Worldwide. And though other countries have played the game well and dominated the sport and have beaten England time and time again, it is still seen as a part of the English culture.

Aside from his experiences with Alan Hemingway and his family, Freddy has seen different aspects of the UK, which have signposted the country for what it is. The scenes and spectacles are endless; however, the Caribbean Diaspora in the UK has managed to forge a continuity of their culture within the British culture.

Chapter 28

Come on England

The last time Freddy counted, there were over forty football clubs that have played in the English Premier League, at one point or another. Extraordinary. Football gone mad. But this is England and a feature of the English society, is the love of football. Though he never played at a major-league level, Freddy has kicked a ball or two in his time, as a young sport enthusiast. The game of football is widely loved by many people in the Caribbean, especially teenage boys.

The love of the game in the Caribbean stems from the popularity of the star-studded Brazilian teams of the 1970s and the players of unbelievable talent of the English teams from the 1960s, coming forward. Banks, Moore, Charlton, Hurst, Robson and more recently, Linekar, Sheringham, Shearer and Gascoigne are some of the names that have become synonymous with football in the Caribbean. Freddy played football with many of the great players of that era and tried to score against Gordon Banks in his high school playground. How so? As boys in high school, there was someone who would take the persona of their favourite player.

The great players of the England 1966 World Cup squad, formed half of his class football team and the Brazilian greats of the 1970 World Cup, formed the other half. Gordon Banks was supposed to be unbeatable in goal and their imitation Gordon Banks saw to that. The Pelé and the Jairzinho had to show that they adopted those names for a reason. They were the kingpins in the playground. They ruled the roost – well - the playground. The fascination with the International football greats, was the same among young boys across all Caribbean Islands.

It was always the dream of many boys who were half good at football, that one day they would play in the English Premier League. The boys in Freddy's secondary school got lucky and they were able to see English football in their school. In their fourth year, the inter-school competition was about to commence and the senior football team was badly in need of a goalkeeper. The coach and everyone else, knew that the current goalkeeper was not up to standard but there was no one else available.

The boys turned up to school one morning and heard that there was a new student who plays football and he was "good". He was from England and he was going to play for the school. He was a goalkeeper. Later that day, they saw him in training. He was brilliant. Freddy and his friends learnt that he was born and raised in

England and his family had moved back to their home in Jamaica; hence the school had that good fortune. The local boys felt as though they had a piece of English football on their turf. The following year, another student arrived from England. He played on the right wing. He was awesome.

A decade or two later and Freddy was now in England and could see English football in front of his very eyes. His first feel of the live football atmosphere was at an under-21 game at West Ham stadium between England and Switzerland. Not a large crowd, by any stretch of the imagination but he was at the stadium where some of the greats that he had heard about two decades earlier, had played.

His generation of football-crazy teenage boys, was not the last. It seems that football-frenzy was in the Caribbean Islands, as much as it exists in England. No one told him how football influenced school work, until he saw the reading material provided for English teaching in British secondary schools. The students studied material about English football players, mangers and championships. The units of work about football went down well with students, who were enthusiasts of the sport and held some of the players as their heroes.

The conversations between Freddy and some of the boys at the schools where he worked in the UK, usually involve the details of their contracts with the Junior division of English Premier League teams. Those with contracts, are given certain afternoons off from school, to go to their club training. It is still only relatively few who get the opportunity to be called up by the big clubs. However, most of the boys who play the game well in school, entertain a strong hope to make it into the Premier League.

To this day, the admiration for the English Premier League, among Caribbean Islanders is as vibrant as it was three, four or five decades ago. Freddy and most members of the Caribbean Diaspora, are asked at one point or another, to take back a football shirt or some memorabilia for a male family member who is keen on the English football Premiership. Freddy has been asked many times by friends in the Caribbean, "Have you been to Manchester United?" "Have you been to Arsenal?"

*****

The England frenzy comes alive during the football season on match days. The frenzy is exercised not only by English nationals but by Diaspora groups from all nationalities. It is common to see the mixed crowds, of all ages, turning out for a match at the Emirates; the home turf of Arsenal football club. A joyous scene as Freddy finds himself caught up in a match-day crowd one Saturday.

As he went through the crowd, he could see a small bright-eyed boy, aged around eight years old, kitted out in his Arsenal home shirt, with the name of his favourite player on the back and player number to finish off. The boy, walking briskly, holds on to his dad's hand while looking up at his sister, who is about age three, who is riding on dad's shoulder, her tiny legs straddling his neck. She is noticeably caught up in the mania, as like her brother, she wears the kit with her favourite player's name and corresponding number. This image has been captured hundreds of times outside football stadiums, in the UK.

This scene embodies the love of football in the social spectrum of the UK. The legacy goes on, as even as the boy walks along and his sister rides on her dad's shoulders, a new generation is being socialised and conditioned for the future. Dad, obviously, has seen the crowds, lived the experience several times and is ensuring that he passes the fever on to his children for continuity. He, at the same time, is decked out in his bigger size shirt - much bigger size - with a name and a number on the back.

It must have been a year or so earlier, when Freddy first heard the frenzied crowds, coming through the exit tunnel of a nearby station, to the Emirates. Arsenal were playing at home. From where he stood, the army of fans oozed out of the tube, for it did have that appearance, from the underground station. They then navigated the twists and turns of the stairways, up to the exit, through another tube-shaped walkway, as though they were being pumped out of a concrete boom and flowed thickly out onto the street.

Now, the crowd was a spectacle in itself. What was also present and carried on with each batch of fans that oozed from the tunnel, thickly, was the incessant singing. Freddy knew not what they were singing. The cacophonous harmony, however, was rousing and turned many heads within earshot. They must have practiced repeatedly, to get the utterances so in-tune. He listened for a good fifteen minutes, using his best word and sound deciphering skills but came up short. Freddy failed to work out what song they were singing and what words were in that song but whatever the words were, the fans knew them all.

As he had to be on his way, to get on and about his business and right up to that point he was none the wiser about the lyrics of the song, he reluctantly sought clarification from a shop keeper who operated on the side of the exit, just outside the station. Freddy chose the shopkeeper as he, Freddy believed, would have heard the song repeatedly on match days. He was right. The shop keeper knew of the song. The shop keeper knew the words of the song too.

"Tell me, what are they singing?" Freddy asked him.

"Who, you mean them?" he replied, ensuring that they were both referring to the same group of people.

"Yes, the people coming out of the tunnel, for the football match," Freddy clarified.

"Arsenal," he said.

"Yes, I know, they are going to Arsenal," Freddy retorted.

"Yes, Arsenal," repeated the shop keeper.

There was by now a slight bit of indignation engulfing Freddy, as at that moment, he realised that there was a problem in communication. He was unsure of the reason, as he felt that he was communicating effectively with the shop keeper. However, Freddy would not give up so easily on this potential source of information, for he needed to know about the song.

By this time, a customer had appeared and the shopkeeper was making the sale of a sausage roll. He opened the hot glassware oven, in which he kept sausage rolls, croissants, pies, saveloys and samosas. After carefully putting the sausage roll in a paper bag and replacing the metal tong he used to grip the item, he folded the top of the bag. before resting it on a napkin and handed it to the customer. The satisfied customer inhaled the aroma, then took a bite, as the shopkeeper handed her back some coins as change.

It was Freddy's turn.

"Do you know the song?" he asked again. "What are they singing?"

"They are singing 'Arsenal', listen," the shopkeeper implored.

"So, what are the other words?" Freddy enquired.

"No other words, just 'Arsenal', took me a while to figure it out myself," he replied, "they are half drunk too."

Well that kind of summed it up. For all of his fascination with the inaudible utterances, Freddy was to find out in one word, what the supporters were singing. The rising sound, followed by the decrescendo of the voices, was quite controlled. Not much can be said though, for the enunciation of the lyrics...or the lack of lyrics, thereof. The only word in that song was 'Arsenal'. They just repeated the word over and over and over until, they believed it was a song. In addition to themselves, they fooled Freddy too.

*****

Having learned his lesson in football for the day, Freddy left the shop and headed out towards the high road. This was a main thorough-fare for the football fans. Lining the streets leading away from the train station, were at least seven police vans. Now these were no ordinary-looking vans. They were shielded at the front by a metal visor, designed with a lattice-like effect. The spaces were, therefore, diamond shaped and small enough to prevent dangerous projectiles from passing through. The spread of the visor was wide enough to shield the entire windscreen from any missile that might be hurled in its direction. These visors could be pulled upwards, depending upon how much protection was needed by the police.

One could not miss the fearsome look of the riot team. Baggy, navy-blue coveralls, with black steel-capped-toe boots. About their waist, were canisters of pepper spray, a night stick hanging loosely, some closed leather pouches and a handcuff. A steely, navy-blue-coloured helmet was worn, with a retractable visor at the front. The helmet was made with an extended protection at the back, to protect the nape. They sat perhaps eight or nine in each van, ready for any eventuality.

Meanwhile, on the outside, on the street, were scores

of other police personnel, dressed in less fearsome fatigue but commanding as much attention, in their high visibility jackets. They could not be missed. They stood eagle-eyed, as the tens, hundreds, even thousands of fans, converged and filed along Blackstock Road, onwards to the Emirates. Well-trained horses stand with riders atop, ready to provide additional rounding up of any trouble-maker who needs to be contained. The occasional siren wails out. Amazingly, shoppers and other pedestrians, who do not form part of the football procession, mix in and out of the football crowd, seemingly unperturbed. After all, they must have seen it all before - numerous times.

It is a way of life. This way of life is replicated in most countries, in the rest of the world. The Caribbean Islands do the same. Spare a thought for the Caribbean teams who have made it into a World Cup final. It is not hard to remember that Jamaica qualified for the finals of the World Cup in 1998 and Trinidad and Tobacco qualified in 2002, for the finals in South Korea and Japan. When Jamaica qualified, a host of second generation, British-born players attended trials for the Jamaica World Cup squad. They were eligible to play for the country of their parents' birth. An opportunity beckoned from their ancestral homeland. At least half a dozen players, born in the UK, made the final squad and flew out with the other *Reggae Boyz* to play in France. On the one hand, they had a desire to fulfil their personal ambitions. On the other hand, they were needed by the *Reggae Boyz*, to add international experience to the squad.

There is no doubt that football connects the UK and the Caribbean countries. The Jamaica *Reggae Boyz* were the darlings of the 1998 World Cup in France. So much so, that at the end of the tournament, an English football club was the first to sign a Jamaican player for the English League.

A good World Cup connoisseur will never forget the fifteen seconds of bold, bustling brilliance that landed the first *Reggae boy* into the English Division one and later, the Premier League. A young nineteen-year-old, named Ricardo Gardener, dazzled the spectators, in a first-round game, in France 1998. Collecting the ball in the centre, he dribbled along, keeping the ball inches away from his feet, deftly turning past the defenders, in a stupendous show of class. Subsequently, Ricardo Gardener was invited to play for Bolton Wanderers Football Club.

The Caribbean Diaspora has had many homegrown and many second-generation players, in English football. Trinidad and Tobago have had players in the Premier League, even before they made it to World Cup 2002. The relationship between the Caribbean Diaspora and English football has carried on long after the 1998 and 2002 tournaments, as by the time World Cup 2014 came around, there were at least six players from the Caribbean Diaspora in the England squad. The England World Cup-winning squad of 1966, was one hundred percent English. More and more players from the Caribbean Diaspora, mainly of Jamaican heritage, are playing in English football leagues.

Britain's love of football is on display weekly, during

the football season. It is evidenced at workplaces, where staff have their regular kick-about. It is evidenced in the school playgrounds, where students hope to be scouted someday, by a Premier League club. It is evidenced in households, where families pledge loyalty to their favourite club.

The interest in football is never confined to English fans, as every nationality in the UK has made the sport their favourite. A walk along the high street, on a match day, tells the story. Some fans who are unable to purchase a match day ticket, or a season ticket, or fans who cannot get time off work, still show their support for their favourite club. Whenever these fans congregate in front of the television at home, at the barber shop or any other venue, the reaction is the same: gasps, cheers, sighs and shouts can be heard for ninety minutes. The noise rises a decibel or two, if the game goes into extra time and goes up a few more decibels, if the game goes to penalty kicks. These fans are passionate.

The Caribbean nations have shown their talent internationally in different sporting events, such as cricket, football, bobsled, and athletics. Dozens of cricketers have been invited to play for English county clubs and many athletes from the Diaspora help to make up the British Athletics team.

Chapter 29

The Movement of the People

Migrants who had made the journey to the UK, had to find a strategy to settle in quickly. The first difference that everyone faces, is the design and location of the houses. The typical British dwelling house is made from bright brownish-red brick. There is little or no difference to be seen between the buildings, from a journey around most communities. A building that houses a family sometimes has the same shape and structural features as a doctor's surgery, a pharmacy, a book shop or a solicitor's office. This was a shock to most migrants arriving from the Caribbean. Anecdotally, some migrants mistook the brownish-red brick buildings for factories, as they looked down from the aircraft upon arrival.

One famous story has been told of a conversation between a new migrant and his relative who had lived in the UK for a while. The new migrant was arriving long before mobile phone image transfer and instant picture messages were in existence and had not seen actual images of buildings in Great Britain. His ambition was to find work quickly, hopefully in a factory. He formed a conclusion about his prospects, as the plane circled over Heathrow airport. The plane continued to circle until the space for landing was ready, as the plane was ten minutes ahead of the scheduled arrival time.

As the Boeing 747 did its in-air manoeuvres, the newly arriving passenger sat in apprehension next to the family member accompanying him.

"There mus be plenty jobs ere," the newly arriving passenger said to his relative.

"Yes, but it depends on what skill you av," replied his relative.

"Oh, well for factory workers dat must be good."

"Yes, many factories deh ere in Inglan," the relative said.

"So, all t'hose buildings 'ar factories down dere?" enquired the rookie.

"No, them ones are mostly houses."

"Oh, I believe dey were factories, look at di colour of di buildings, an dey joined up an dey av smoke comin from the roof; dat looks like when work is goin on inside a factory," the newly arriving migrant concluded.

Smiling, his relative explained, "No, most buildings are made from bricks and dey mostly join' up alongside the road."

"Oh, I see," said the new migrant.

"The 'smoke' you see is the steam dat is coming from di chimneys. The houses av a boiler dat give off steam when it is workin," explained the seasoned Brit.

The protégée had a look of bewilderment at what he just heard. At the same time, he had the obvious look of disappointment, as he thought that his prospect of a factory work was now calamitously diminished.

But who could blame this traveller for his conclusion, as he looked down from the plane over Heathrow? For he knew that in the Caribbean, buildings were clearly designed for different purposes and most were stand-alone units, with acres of land around them; especially in the rural areas. The houses were built with a design of their owners' choice as that was allowed. The potential home owner had the choice to build on land bought or inherited and so the design was a matter of personal taste. Most houses in the Caribbean, especially in the suburban and rural areas, boasted a boundary clearly demarcated with flowers, a wall or a fence. The space in the front yard could be large enough to comfortably fit half a dozen cars.

The contrast between that Caribbean description and the design and layout of houses in the UK is striking. Houses in the UK are joined along a high street, for up to ten units attached, followed by a narrow gap. Following the narrow gap, another ten or more houses will follow to the end of the road. This is the typical high street or side street lay out of houses in the cities and this is the most common type of accommodation for the migrants from the Caribbean. Hence, this is the first noticeable difference for the Diaspora to come to terms with.

The large front yard, as was commonly seen in the

Caribbean has disappeared in Great Britain. The houses along the high road in London and many other cities in the UK, have a space to accommodate a wheelie bin or two and sometimes three: a bin for household waste, sometimes a bin for cuttings from the garden and a bin for recycling. Alas, it could be two sets of bins if the lot number is shared by two separate households. This is a common feature of city dwelling in the UK. A newly arriving migrant might not immediately occupy or own a house with a large front yard, capable of fitting four cars, let alone one car. Perhaps, there is space suitable for one bicycle.

A migrant who owns a car in the UK certainly has to come to terms with some unfamiliar locations for a car repair shop. Freddy was first directed to a car mechanic in the East side of London, White Chapel. He pulled up next to the train station and wondered if the mechanic was getting off the train to meet him. He had heard of mobile mechanics who drive around in a van, with their tools and turn up when called. On this occasion, Freddy wondered if this was an on-call train-hopping mechanic who would meet him at the station, with his tool kit. He would soon find out.

The mechanic was under the railway arch. He worked there. There were raised concrete walls where the train line crossed over the adjacent road. There was a series of stone arches resulting from this raised section and the mechanic had his workshop beneath the train line. Freddy was one of about four other customers waiting to be served. As he stood beneath the railway arch, he could only admire the innovative use of these train arches to provide this service. Some other arches under this bridge were used for furniture making and other consumer services. To complete the picture, the auto-repair shop has a metal shutter at its entrance, so the vehicles are unexposed at night. This was such a contrast to the local mechanic in the Caribbean.

The regular, friendly, community mechanic could be seen running his business at his gate or in his yard in the Caribbean. A large mango tree or guinep tree provided enough shade for his mechanic workshop. The branches on the tree - for they were strong trees - were used as beams to support ropes and pulleys, that were tied and suspended. These suspended ropes were then used for hoisting engines out of cars. Then there were those cars too sick to be repaired. Rest assured, they would remain on the premises for weeks, months and sometimes years. Engine and body parts would be gradually removed to restore life to other cars that were in need of repairs. There were no train arch garages.

The outward appearance of schools was another source of alarm for the Diaspora from the Caribbean Islands. Schools were clearly situated along roads with a wall running along the roadway in the Caribbean. A mural sometimes was painted on the out-facing side of that wall. Most secondary schools were two or three storeys high. It was common sight to go past a secondary school in Jamaica for instance, and see students walking on corridors; three floors up in the air. The inner side of the corridor had classrooms running along the length of the block. Classrooms on the upstairs only had a hand-rail running along on the open side for the length of the block. The pride of each school was displayed in its colour. Blue buildings meant that the uniform worn by the students was predominantly blue. Burgundy buildings meant that burgundy was the predominant colour of the uniform. The corridor rails also bore the paint of the school colours.

Freddy and the other Millennial migrant teachers especially, quickly realised that not only was the appearance of buildings, colour of external walls and layout of schools different from what they were used to but the administration of the schools was also different. A new student from the Caribbean Islands had to grapple with these differences too.

A student who arrives from the Caribbean, upon enrolment in schools in the UK, is invariably placed in a low ability group. The practice has been repeated in a number of schools, as the Jamaican teachers who work in the British schools have attested to the prevalence of this reality. On most occasions, these Caribbean students soon prove that they are as academically astute as their British counterparts and the GCSE results usually confirm it.

Behaviour in schools in the UK is significantly different from the acceptable forms of behaviour in secondary schools in the Caribbean. The Millennial teachers in secondary schools in the UK will have lost count of the number of times a student was heard swearing in the corridor or in the playground. Furthermore, most teachers, especially in London, will be able to relate an instance, or two, or three, when they have been sworn at in the classroom. Usually, there are no real measures to end this undesirable practice, for the punitive measures being used are ineffective for the most part.

The views expressed by teachers and other stakeholders who have seen both sides of the classroom experience are the same. The consensus is that there is a greater appreciation for teachers in other parts of the world, especially in the Caribbean. The generally high level of respect for teachers stems from the long-standing tradition of parent/teachers' associations. This fosters a strong collaboration between teachers and parents who meet regularly. Both parents and teachers come to understand and support the effort of the other in a joint cause; there is mutual respect as they work together to provide the best academic and vocational opportunities for the students. The professionals who have seen both sides of the school system also believe that the absence of many second chances in the Caribbean Islands, means that students focus on their work and try to do their best at the first opportunity.

The movement of the Caribbean people into the UK means that adjustments have to be made all the time. The Caribbean migrants who keep dogs as pets, had to make an adjustment for these animals in the UK. The UK dog has clothes made specifically to be worn in the winter. The dog is also part of the family and shares the house with the rest of family. Within the home, there is the dog's sleeping quarters. The dog usually has its bath in the family bath, shares the owners' bed in some cases, and goes on holidays with the family. This is in contrast to the place of dogs in the Caribbean Islands, where dogs are kept in kennels built outside in the yard. The kinder weather, however, makes this possible for a dog in the Caribbean. A dog would have severe difficulties sleeping outdoors in a kennel in two-degrees Celsius temperature in the British winter.

Finally, the United Kingdom is renowned for its stable democracy and the cordial nature of its political process. In Jamaica for instance, a migrant, especially from the Twentieth Century, will know of turbulent pre-election and post-election periods in that country. As a kind of unusual custom, the national elections for members of parliament and prime ministers are usually very visible affairs. For several months building up to a national election, there is frequent large gatherings of supporters from both major political parties. These are enormous gatherings which could be up to ten thousand supporters in one town square, all in one specific evening.

Prior to the meeting, the key organisers from the political party would arrange for dozens of trucks, buses and minivans to be available. These vehicles take supporters from different points around the country and transport them into the main town square. The political candidate then turns up and makes his speech and as the rally goes on, supporters will find whatever vantage point there is available. This could be on top of shops, on vehicles and from windows of buildings within the vicinity. Colours were the identifying feature of the crowd with each of the two major parties, having its own signifier. The respective colours were worn as a mark of allegiance to a political party. The rally, as they were frequently called, was not complete without singing and chanting to the accompaniment of whistles, bells and horns.

The Political landscape of Great Britain takes on a tone and flavour which is quite different from that of the Caribbean. The Caribbean Diaspora in Great Britain had to adjust to the difference. The national elections are relatively quiet affairs in the UK. Without the broadcasts from the news network channels and social media, an election in the UK could pass by without much visible Ado.

After living through nearly two decades in the UK and several elections to go with it, Freddy is yet to see a motorcade of ten thousand participants dressed in a colour to represent a political party, heading up the high road for a four-hour rally in the night. A few day time trips do occur. Those seeking political office will turn up to job sites and community centres in different cities around the country to push their political manifesto in the UK.

With such a difference in the pre-election build-up and campaigning in the UK, it must have taken some time for the Diaspora from the Caribbean to adjust to the British approach to national elections. The chances of seeing lorry loads of voters and hearing singing to horns, drums and bells in the UK, would be non-existent.

With differences in national elections aside, there had to be an adjustment to the stoic nature of the British public. The Caribbean way of life is generally friendly, accommodating and congruous. It is common practice in the Caribbean to greet others in the day to day commute. The greetings naturally evolve into conversation. It is generally acceptable for two travellers at a bus stop or at any point of meeting, to say some form of greeting to each other. Greetings will range from the formal "Good morning", to the more informal, "How you do?" to the more casual, "Bless Up", or "Everything good?" But whatever the circumstances, a greeting would be expected. Some members of the Diaspora have tried to greet fellow passengers from different ethnicities at the bus stop, or on the roads, upon arrival in the UK. The responses to the greetings have not been the same as in the Caribbean.

The adjustment to the British way of life has been quite difficult for some migrants. To work around this, many migrants re-create the Caribbean lifestyle as much as possible within the UK. Diaspora groups from other parts of the world do the same as they co-exist with "Britishness". What is "Britishness"? The answer varies from place to place and takes the view of the individual who gives the definition. The answers usually include:

"Britishness is to do with the Queen and the Royal Family"

"Britishness is fish and chips"

"Britishness is the pound sterling"

"Britishness is the flag"

"Britishness is having a stiff upper lip"

"Britishness is football"

"Britishness is Loyalty to Queen and country"

"Britishness is about the Beatles"

"Britishness is drinking tea"

"Britishness is James Bond"

"Britishness is the pub and Sunday roast"

"Britishness is the full English breakfast".

The Diaspora groups still carry on with their day to day activities as best as they can. The Caribbean Diaspora quickly find ways and means to exist within the British society and make adjustments to "Britishness".

Chapter 30

Lost in Transit

It is not unusual to get lost in a new place. There is a feeling of fright and dismay that comes with being lost and the feeling is the same for a starry-eyed student who gets lost in a new school or an adult who gets lost at a new workplace or in a new city. The schoolboy usually goes through a ritual the night before the first day of his new school and he still gets lost. The thoughts of the night before may run like a rehearsal:

Now I have my bag ready with pencils, pens, sharpener, PE kit, my diary and snacks. Let me see, I will set my alarm for 6:30, mom and dad won't even be awake at that time. I am going to have my bath and put my clothes on before they wake up. Ah, I can turn the telly on in my room and watch my morning programme. Great. That will help me to keep calm, before I leave out for

*school. I will make sure at school that I pay
attention to my new timetable and learn where
the classrooms are. I don't want to be lost. Oh,
the toilets are very important, so I will know and
remember where to find those too. I learnt how to
find my way around my primary school so it
should be fine in secondary school. Well, I think I
will go to my bed now, I don't want to be too tired
in the morning. What can possibly go wrong?*

However, he turns up to the new school - big school -
on the first day and the rehearsal does not go to plan.
Little girls and boys will soon find that the new school
is quite complicated. Negotiating the many blocks,
stairs, classrooms, Science labs, Computer labs, Music
and Technology rooms, becomes daunting and
sometimes leads to an overwhelming frustration,
apathy and occasionally, tears.

Freddy had his share of anguish and apathy like the
schoolboy, when he got lost in London. Most of the
streets looked similar and that caused his predicament.

As someone who had just arrived in London, Freddy
was about to experience the difficulty of driving around
in a strange place. He and his colleagues who had
arrived in the New Millennium knew the streets of
Jamaica well but moving to London took them out of
their comfort zone. Freddy had to travel across the city,
from East London to West London without the use of a
road map or a satellite navigation system, one late
afternoon. London has a unique geographical layout.
The four divisions make it seem easy to navigate. Cross

the River Thames northbound, go straight ahead and you are in North London. Cross the River Thames southbound and you are in South London. That sounds pretty straight forward and a matter of logical deduction. With some knowledge of the compass directions, a traveller in London could then work out that arriving north of the river and going to the left will lead to West London. Cross the Thames northbound then venture to the right and that should lead to East London.

How difficult then could it be to head into West London from East London and back? This is the question that Freddy learnt the answer for, with a great deal of stress. When he and his friends decided to leave Stratford, late evening, to get a new car from a dealer in the west of London, it seemed a simple matter to accomplish. They had the service of an old blue Vauxhall Astra, which in all fairness, was quite dependable. It needed a bit of care but without complaining, it took the owner from place to place. This blue Vauxhall Astra would take three of them across the city centre to West London. Two of them would ride back in the Astra and one person would drive the newly purchased Vauxhall Vectra, back to East London. Simple. What could go wrong?

There was still a bit of light left in the evening sky when Freddy and his colleagues, Stephanie and Leighton, set out from Stratford. The normal evening traffic rolled on along Bow Road. The route was punctuated by number 25 buses, that run westward into Oxford Circus. The journey was a stop start affair.

To add to the slow pace of travel, a temporary set of traffic lights were in place at a junction that was previously serviced by a normal set of lights. It is hard to understand why a set of temporary traffic lights can never be set with the same timings as the lights that they replace and there is always a major traffic snarl, wherever lights have been set up temporarily at road junctions in London. So, they waited for what seemed like hours to get beyond that badly-timed traffic regulatory device.

A little while later and Freddy, Stephanie and Leighton were in the heart of the city. The night time lighting of the city can be a delightful spectacle to view. Towering buildings, unusual street names, a range of shops, artistic displays in windows, electronic billboards - changing all the time - each page presenting a different product or a service or an entertainment event. On this particular evening, with the sunlight leaving the skyline, the centre of the city was not the place that Freddy and his friends wanted to be. They were on a journey. A journey across the city. With more traffic delays, they belatedly got away from the city centre and made their way slowly, but steadily, along Westway. They finally got to the car shop, in the narrowest margin of time before the shop closed. The new car was there – ready and waiting.

With payments confirmed and documents handed over, it was time to get back on the road, across the city and into the East End of town, with a new set of wheels. Freddy assumed the role of lead driver. Heading out through the gates and onto the high street, the automatic power of the Vauxhall Vectra added pleasure to the driving experience. He remembered the route well - or so he thought. Freddy exited Wood Lane, onto Westway, enroute to central London; or so he thought. The traffic was beyond heavy. It was a parking lot. Night, by this time, had put in its appearance. Headlights were illuminating from all directions, as vehicles lined the street eastwards and westwards on the dual carriage way. There were headlights to be seen on side streets leading onto Westway too. A close estimate of progress on either side of the motor way, was about five miles per hour; bearing in mind that such an estimate is quite lenient.

*****

As he was the sole occupant of the Vauxhall Vectra, Freddy tuned into *drive time* radio for company; some kind of paradox he thought, as very little driving was taking place. The song that he heard as he tuned in to *drive time* radio was by Daniel Powter: '*Bad Day*'.

"What!" Freddy said to himself.

The song was a bad selection.

"This is a conspiracy," he thought.

It was unfortunate enough to be having a bad day, or more precisely, a bad night, in traffic. He could do without the reminder from the radio.

"What will they play next?" he wondered.

If the ill-timed songs were going to keep coming, he

anticipated something along the lines of '*Night Shift*', by the Commodores. If that had happened, he would be convinced that the radio presenter was making fun of his predicament. Freddy concluded that '*Coming in from the Cold*', by Bob Marley would have been the best of bad choices, under those circumstances.

*****

The movement along the road was notoriously slow. From Freddy's calculation, the journey in one direction was thirteen miles and should be completed in approximately fifty-five minutes. It was approaching an hour since they left the car shop and inching along but still had not reached Central London. Freddy's lead car crept along a bit more but still no familiar sightings along the way. This was becoming uncomfortably long. With *drive time* radio adding insult to injury, he made a phone call to the rest of his party in the blue Vauxhall Astra behind him. They were following his lead. The Vectra he was driving was white with 15-inch alloys and a 2Litre engine. Enough said then, for power. Power which served no purpose at that moment.

His party was less troubled as being two together in that vehicle, they had taken less notice of the actual distance they had travelled, without seeing the familiar sights of Central London. At this point, Freddy decided to take matters into the outside world. Rolling the window down, he enquired of the driver in the car adjacent to his, for a journey estimate.

"Hello, excuse me," he said to the driver, who seemed more relaxed than Freddy was.

The driver looked across at him in acknowledgement and so Freddy continued to probe for direction.

"Can you tell me how far we are from Central London?" asked Freddy.

"Central London?" repeated the driver, with some degree of consternation. "It's that way," indicating by his thumb that Central London was behind Freddy.

How could that be? Looking at Freddy, the other driver must have seen the bewildered look of a school boy on his first day at school, who thought he had marked all the buildings, but inevitably got lost on the corridors.

"Where are you going?" the driver asked, sensing that this 'schoolboy' was lost.

"Stratford," Freddy replied, at least he was sure of that.

"You are far away; you will have to turn back at the next roundabout."

"Where is that?" Freddy enquired.

"Hangar Lane," said the driver.

At that point, Freddy remembered hearing of a place called Hangar lane, since the time he arrived in the UK. Hangar Lane, from what he heard, was almost a synonym for, 'a driver's nightmare in peak hour travel'. He was now living that nightmare.

"When you get to Hangar Lane, be careful," the driver cautioned, "there are several exits so you need to go all the way around and come back this way on the other side of Westway."

That was some parting shot, as the other driver's side of traffic moved ahead of Freddy's. Fear mounted with that warning as another wrong choice of road could mean an unwanted night on the town after a long day.

Sensing the quandary, they were in, Freddy rang back his colleagues in the blue Vauxhall Astra. He advised them to keep as close as possible as they approached Hangar Lane. An hour and a half after leaving the car shop, they arrived at Hangar Lane and successfully negotiated the exits. They were on the way back to the East side. Half an hour later, they wearily got into Central London. Another thirty minutes after and they were cruising back along Bow Road in East London. They all knew the East London streets well. The new 2Litre Vauxhall Vectra, with 15-inch alloys, was humming confidently along the road into Stratford. The two-and-a-half-hour journey, which should have taken fifty-five minutes, had delayed testing out the quality of the Vectra's high-performance engine. Back now, into Stratford, around the high street and up onto Romford Road, they went. By this time, it was way into the night; a mission accomplished, after much confusion.

So, what became of the Vauxhall Astra? Although being close to performing its last set of rites, it held on for a few more months. When it got to its last knees, it was sold on to the dismantlers. The Vauxhall Vectra kept busy for a few more years, before being relegated to another league. For how much longer it continued in the starting eleven, no one knows.

*****

Freddy has tried to avoid the Hangar Lane vicinity as much as he can, ever since that night. There is no joy in that memory of taking the wrong way to find home. From the travail of that night, he could empathise with the student in a new school who finds it difficult to negotiate the blocks without getting lost. Hangar Lane still causes a bit of trepidation each time Freddy goes near that side of town. However, perhaps this serves as a watershed moment, for the man who came to London...

* The End *

About the author

A. S. Cookson is currently a Teacher of English and a former Head of Drama. He is a member of *Cambridge English Teacher* and the *Society for Education and Training* and has a MA level degree in Communication, Media and Public Relations, from the University of Leicester.

The author has previously volunteered with a project to develop English Education in the South East Asian region. He has written journals and marketing content for an International College website.

Aside from writing, A. S. Cookson has a passion for comedy, performing arts and cricket. He currently lives with his wife, Sandra, in London, UK.

Useful links

---

https://www.theguardian.com/education/2015/oct/11/agency-hires-jamaican-teachers-for-english-schools

http://news.bbc.co.uk/1/hi/education/1871706.stm

http://www.nytimes.com/2008/11/09/travel/09Jamaica.html

http://www.express.co.uk/entertainment/books/501998/James-Bond-author-Ian-Fleming-facts

http://www.bbc.co.uk/news/uk-14436499

http://www.independent.co.uk/life-style/food-and-drink/features/caribbean-cuisine-is-becoming-increasingly-popular-in-the-uk-and-theres-more-to-it-than-jerk-chicken-9698009.html

http://jamaica-gleaner.com/gleaner/20100505/news/news9.html

http://www.newsamericasnow.com/10-fast-facts-about-caribbean-immigrants-in-the-uk/

Focus group questions

_____

As with most literary works that explore matters surrounding people and their culture, this book may raise a number of potential open-ended discussion points. The following questions could elicit a range of points of view for personal reflection or for discussion in focus groups.

1. The dogs present a sense of fear and intimidation as Freddy comes through Heathrow airport.
- What are your views on the prolific use of sniffer dogs, especially for flights from Jamaica?

2. How likely is it that the barber shop will continue to be a cultural meeting place for the Jamaican Diaspora?

3. Is the presentation of the British classroom, as experienced by Freddy, Dean, and Miss Johnson, a realistic description, or a gross exaggeration?

4. Miss Johnson seems stunned by Katie's comments in chapter 8 - "A Jamaican in England teaching English?"
- What discussion would you have had with Miss Johnson, if you were there at that moment?

- How do you think she will relay this incident to her colleagues back in the Caribbean?

5. In chapter 9, Dean is shocked by his unexpected promotion. What do you think were the immediate thoughts going through his mind?

6. In chapter 14, do you think Mr Steele is aware that the students have little or no understanding of *post-traumatic stress disorder*?

7. How do you think the students would have treated Mr Steele had they had a clear understanding of *post-traumatic stress disorder*?

8. What do you think happened with Sonia, in the months and years after she returned from Iraq?

9. With reference to chapters 16 and 17, to what extent does the exposure to International cultures affect the Caribbean culture?

10. What are your views on Bob (chapter 21), and the boys in school and the impact of migration on their relationship?

   - What do you think the future holds for Bob?

11. Freddy 'discovers' some interesting facts while on "The road trip". How significant are these 'discoveries' for a Millennial migrant from the

Caribbean?

12. In chapters 26, modern-day technology has made migration more bearable. To what extent do you agree?

13. Can you argue for or against the changing face of British sports teams in the light of migration from the Caribbean and other parts of the world?

14. Of the differences cited in chapter 29, what are the most difficult ones for a Caribbean migrant to adjust to?

15. Going by the title of the book, what are some of the reasons for Caribbean nationals to migrate to the UK in the Twenty-first Century?

Study Notes

....
....
....
....
....
....
....
....
....
....
....
....
....
....
....
....
....
....
....
....
....
....

....

....

....

....

....

....

....

....

....

....

....

....

....

....

....

....

....

....

....

....

....

....

....

Lightning Source UK Ltd.
Milton Keynes UK
UKHW02f0605160318
319518UK00003B/21/P